2 6.B

Beth Russell's
TRADITIONAL NEEDLEPOINT

Beth Russell's
TRADITIONAL
NEEDLEPOINT

BETH RUSSELL

Photography by
JOHN GREENWOOD

•

"My work is the embodiment of dreams
in one form or another . . ."
WILLIAM MORRIS, 1856

The Readers Digest Association, Inc.
Pleasantville, New York · Montreal

For Peter, Nick and Sam,
Paul and Julie

Photography by John Greenwood
Photographic styling by Andrea Spencer

Library of Congress Cataloging in Publication Data

Russell, Beth.
    [Traditional needlepoint]
    Beth Russell's traditional needlepoint/Beth Russell.
        p.   cm.
    "A David & Charles book"—T.p. verso.
    Includes bibliographical references and index.
    ISBN 0-89577-446-1
    1. Canvas embroidery—England—Patterns.   2. Decoration and
ornament—Plant forms—England.   I. Title.   II. Title: Traditional
needlepoint.
TT778.C3R87 1992
746.44'2041—dc20   92-17581

CONTENTS

INTRODUCTION

EMBROIDERY IS A WAY of life for me: it is both my work and my joy. It can be a wonderful source of companionship, of sharing and comparing experiences and experiments with friends. At times it can be so totally absorbing that being alone is a pleasure.

Driving home on a bleak day is one of the times that I most relish the thought of returning to my stitching. The anticipation of a warm room, a cozy chair, and a challenging design cancels all the frustrations of the day. As I make the first stitch, all the thoughts, dreams, hopes, and happenings of the previous stitching flood my mind as if they were woven into the embroidery itself and are once again released.

Beth Russell as a child in Welsh costume.

•

A WELSH CHILDHOOD

Memories of my life as a young girl in South Wales conjure up feelings of complete security: a calm, kind mother, a warm welcoming kitchen smelling of fresh-baked bread, coal fires, freezing bathrooms, back doors that were never locked, popping into neighbors' homes for tea and Welsh cakes. Security meant feeling totally free to run in the fields . . . to climb fences, trees, hills . . . and to spend hours underneath a wheelbarrow waiting for the rain, to see if my makeshift house was waterproof. In the evenings, I would watch my father paint in oils or watercolors, make furniture, satchels, and even shoes; at Christmas he made the best consommé I've ever tasted. I shared a private world of creativity within the home, complemented by the freedom to explore the world outside.

Much has happened since then, but I think the emotional freedom that I had as a child gave me the confidence to experiment. My own methods tend to be somewhat unconventional: my instinct is to try something first and take lessons later. However, in this book, I offer the best technical advice that I can find from experts. This, combined with my enthusiasm for experimentation, will hopefully furnish you with some of the tools to embark on your own projects. My reluctance to give instructions for certain things, such as upholstering, is not because I have never tried it, but because my methods are rather individual and, I am quite sure, not always the easiest! Although I retain the desire to explore and to challenge my own abilities, I still seek the creative perfection that my father cherished.

LIFE ON THE THAMES

My present location is far away from my beginnings. These days I live high up, overlooking the River Thames, and my days are dominated by the sun. In the winter it rises and sets within our line of vision, and when it shines, it stays with us all day.

My "second" family lives here in this urban environment, so they are not blessed with the freedom that I had. However, we are compensated by the space we see, the variety of our careers, and the common interests we share.

Every member of my family has a role in our company, Designers Forum. My husband Peter, my sons Nick and Paul, and my daughter-in-law Julie take care of the business side. My brother Roy Haynes gives us sound business advice, and my other daughter-in-law, Sam, pops in to lend a hand when we need her.

I am left free to indulge my addiction for new designs. My time may be spent drawing, coloring, or visiting libraries and museums. Whenever we can, Peter and I travel to one of the famous William Morris or De Morgan houses, which are such good sources of inspiration. I may need to go to one of my stitchers to see how a sample is coming along. However much preliminary stitching I have done, the work tends to be rather like a scrapbook or sketch pad, and only when the parts of the design are seen in their relevant places, surrounded by background, can the true effect be judged. Every day I try to stitch a little myself, checking how colors blend together and how subtle shapes can be formed and brought to life on a rigid medium such as canvas.

I always have a stack of new designs either in my head, half-drawn, or partly stitched. My itch to try the latest design in new colors, with a different background, or to a different scale – even before the first sample has been completed – sometimes makes it difficult to concentrate on one thing at a time.

I love the family feeling of what I do, not only working with my immediate family, but also enjoying close friendship with and helpful advice from many people who are more experienced in draftsmanship and needlepoint than I, and who are brilliant technicians who interpret my ideas into beautiful reality.

•

Working on African Marigold in my London studio.

DESIGNERS FORUM

From the outset I wanted Designers Forum to gain a reputation for excellence and quality. The source of my work is arguably the richest period in the history of British design, both in the number of great designers and in the brilliance of their workmanship. My aim is to remain true to the essence of their designs, even though I change the medium with which to display them. My firm belief is that it is foolish to work with inferior materials; my father's voice saying "If a job is worth doing, it's worth doing well" was heard too frequently for me not to believe it. Time and creativity are more valuable than the canvas and threads and should not be wasted working with materials that will neither do justice to your efforts nor last long enough to hand down to your grandchildren.

So all Designers Forum kits contain the best canvas that we can find and are hand printed by a perfectionist craftsman. The superb color selection of Appleton yarn provides a wealth of choice with which to echo the designs I love.

THE JOY OF STITCHERY

If you have never felt the secret joy of watching your design grow and evolve as you work, then I hope that this book will persuade you either to start stitching or – if you have already – to enjoy it even more. You will hopefully find not just designs to copy, but ideas to inspire. Once you are thoroughly involved with stitching, you can stretch your talents to the full – your sense of color, style, and texture, your ability to shade and shape – you should feel confident and

*The Jackfield Rose design shown in
tent stitch for a picture and in cross stitch
for a tablecloth.*

•

*The Pomegranate rug. Its variety
of color and lovely curves are typical of
Morris's work.*

•

free to interpret as you wish, to show what you genuinely see. You will be surprised as you unlock these hidden talents. New worlds of color and shape will unfold. Stitching, like music or painting, involves a flow and a rhythm which are both personal and universal, creating a therapeutic peacefulness.

We all see things slightly differently; color particularly affects us in different ways. It is constantly fascinating to see how quickly some people can choose colors to blend and harmonize. This gift can, to a certain extent, be learned. The more often color decisions are made, the easier they are.

In this book I try to show the enormous variety of uses to which charts can be put. By changing the materials used – the gauge of canvas, the type of stitch, the colors – you will find that the same design allows you to produce an enormous number of beautiful and quite different works of art. Part of a design can be used for a single delicate picture; a pillow can be enlarged into a rug, or a rug can be reduced to a pillow. What is shown or discussed should be just the start of your experiments with charts. I hope to show the way – you can then exercise your own inspiration, tastes, and needs to move ahead into your own world of artistry.

I hope that this book will provide not just the key to a door, but also a travel guide to the unexplored continent of your own abilities.

Author's Note: The designs in this book were stitched using Appleton yarns. The Paternayan yarns given are not exact equivalents in color, and the quantities stated are estimates only.

THE ARTS & CRAFTS MOVEMENT

MY FASCINATION with the designs of William Morris remains intact after many years. The more familiar I become with them, the more enthusiastic I feel. His aims in life and in work were impeccable, and his creativity seems to have been infectious. Every so often, history reports on groups of close friends who were renowned for their talents, but seldom can there have been a group displaying such a variety of skills – all of a style, all complementary, yet all so individual – as the Arts & Crafts Movement. The artist Dante Gabriel Rossetti, the painter Edward Burne-Jones, the architect Philip Webb, and William De Morgan, the designer of ceramics and stained glass, remained lifelong friends of Morris. Many others throughout the world also helped to provide us with the wealth of controversial yet enduring designs that were created during this period.

It is interesting to learn how the paths of so many gifted men in this time of great change and creativity crossed with Morris. Fascinating, too, is how an interest in a certain style or fashion can take root simultaneously in different people and different countries – this style had a lot of its roots in the East.

THE GREAT EXHIBITION

The International Exhibition held in London in 1862 created enormous interest throughout Europe. For the first time Morris, Marshall & Faulkner (The Firm) exhibited its designs, inspired mainly by the art of the Middle Ages. Included were a sofa by Rossetti, a washstand by Webb, and tiles designed by both of them as well as by Burne-Jones and Morris. There was stained glass, embroideries, and furniture, and although the designs were criticized by many of

A small section of the wallhanging embroidered by Morris himself in 1857. It is stitched in wool yarn on linen, using a relatively unknown and difficult stitch which we are told Morris was determined to master. The original now hangs in Kelmscott Manor.

•

the traditionalists, they won two gold medals and enjoyed a successful launch.

Just as significant – if not more so – was a Japanese section. Japan had not traded with Europe before, and the Exhibition provided the first glimpse that most visitors had ever experienced of the simple elegance of Japanese style. Its total contrast to Victorian fashion caused great excitement. At the close of the exhibition, the unsold pieces were bought to form the basis of an Oriental Warehouse in the West End of London, to be managed by Arthur Lasenby Liberty, future owner of the world-famous department store in Regent Street. He became an expert in Oriental fabrics, and, when he opened his own store in 1875, it became a meeting place for the cognoscenti of the time. Liberty Art Silks, soft in both texture and color, were received enthusiastically over by many, including Morris, Rossetti, and Burne-Jones. Oriental artifacts from furniture to jewelry were to be found there. This new fashion was light-years away from the neon-colored needlepoint and heavy, stiff brocades that typified Victoriana.

When Arthur Lasenby Liberty decided to produce his own collection of fabrics, he turned to Thomas Wardle, who is better known as Morris's chief dyer. Later, both Morris and Liberty had their own dyeing facilities on

London's River Wandle, taking advantage of the soft water which was particularly suitable for dyeing fabrics with madder and other natural substances. Morris was at Merton Abbey; Liberty was upstream from him. William De Morgan, who had found the premises for Morris, moved close by just a year later in 1882.

C. F. A. Voysey (1875–1941) was an architect and interior designer, as well as a creator of furniture, wallpaper, textiles, and metalwork. In many of the houses that he built, he was responsible – like Morris – for all the details, from fireplaces to windows. His greatest influences were Arthur McMurdo and Morris, and his love of Japanese art was incorporated into his distinctive simple linear style. He, too, was commissioned to produce designs for Liberty.

William De Morgan met Morris in 1863, at the age of 24, and remained a lifelong friend. He abandoned his studies in Fine Arts at London's Royal Academy and became a devotee of the decorative arts. Best known for his ceramic tiles, he also produced stained glass, pottery, paintings, and furniture; in later life, like Morris, he wrote books. He was a chemist as well as an artist and understood the techniques of glazing and firing so well that he was able to match exactly the Isnik tiles to complete an Islamic scheme commissioned by Lord Leighton, which can still be seen today at the magnificent Leighton House Museum in London. Certainly some of De Morgan's tiles have an Eastern flavor, but his work is highly individual, encompassing beauty, humor and terror (rather like the stories of Roald Dahl). Some of the animals he depicts are fascinatingly grotesque, his peacocks sumptuous, and his owls gently amusing. Other fine collections of his work are at the Debenham House, in Addison Road, and the Victoria & Albert Museum, both in the same area of London as Leighton House.

My lasting affection for the styles of the period was initiated by the inspiring Brangwyn Panels in Swansea,

The William Morris room in the superb showrooms of Arthur Sanderson & Sons in London, showing a very small selection of their current line of Morris fabrics and wallpapers available for sale. Overseen by a portrait of Morris himself are one of the original pear-wood printing blocks, a current Sanderson hand-blocked wallpaper pattern book, "Vine" and "Chrysanthemum" in tapestry-weave upholstery fabric, hand-blocked "Trellis" wallpaper, and "Marigold," both on the wall and in the foreground.

•

Wales, which I first saw on my seventh birthday. Frank Brangwyn was another whose life touched Morris; he was apprenticed to him in 1882. His style of painting is so distinctive that I believe I would recognize it anywhere. Early in 1991, on vacation on the island of Bali, my husband and I "discovered" an octogenarian Balinese whose paintings were so like those of Brangwyn that it quite stunned me. Brangwyn had traveled extensively, and his style, too, must surely have been influenced by that of the East.

So all the threads that tie this book together meet. I feel privileged to have been born in a country with such a rich heritage and to be able to perpetuate the work of so many great talents. Their legacy will live forever. To re-create it in our own homes is both beautiful and rewarding.

What business have we with art at all, unless we can share it?
WILLIAM MORRIS

One of the many original Morris & Co. wallpaper printing logs now owned by Arthur Sanderson & Sons and held in their design archive outside London.

COMPTON

Ompton is the largest and most dramatic rug that I have ever attempted – its slow evolution was so enjoyable that I could hardly bear to finish it! But I have always been attracted to partially worked designs. The gentle movement of the background through this design is like the sea moving up and down the beach and changing the color of the sand. I love to remember how it looked in its early stages.

The original design was created as a wallpaper and textile by Morris & Company in 1896 and destined for Compton Hall, Wolverhampton. All the hallmarks of William Morris are here; the bold flowers catch your attention, but do not overpower the wonderful detail – the balance of design and background is perfect.

Arthur Sanderson & Sons of London is the owner of all of Morris & Company's original woodblocks for printing wallpaper, and they still produce many designs by hand-blocking in the traditional way. Some, like Compton, have been transferred to machine to provide a more economical range of both wallpapers and fabrics. Interestingly, the design was reduced for machine, and when I enlarged it to accommodate the delicate shapes on an 8#/inch (3#/cm) rug canvas, I unknowingly returned it almost to its original proportions. As I wanted the rug to look right from every angle, I also had to give it a center and reverse the design at each end. The original, of course, all lies in one direction – it also repeats – so the rug needed a natural ending all around. Thanks to the fine draftsmanship of Phyllis Steed, this has been achieved without detracting from the beauty of a timeless classic.

My first intention was to add a decorative border, using some of the central design and adapting it, but after studying the first drawings this seemed inappropriate. The center is so strong that an extra border would just look fussy. So I stitched a plain black border to give the effect of framing the rug and emphasizing the center.

The background to the central design was a problem. I felt that black was too sharp and charcoal was too blue – so, in the end, charcoal, very dark green, and brown were blended. This may seem fussy, but it achieved the color I wanted. Let's hope that you (and Morris!) approve.

The rug led naturally to the big pillow. It is worked on finer canvas, but it had to be large enough to stand up to the impact of the rug. It uses just one end of the rug design,

•

The Compton rug, seen here nearing completion, with its companion pillow and (overleaf) in use. The two photographs help to illustrate wonderfully the true strength of this design; it blends with the elegance of a carpeted room as easily as it reflects the warmth and drama of the inglenook fireplace and stone floor.

adapted to finish neatly at the top and bottom. Some of the smaller blue flowers have been omitted, as they looked unbalanced.

I know of two people who have adapted the rectangular pillow into square ones, using printed canvases and stitching just the red and pink flowers and the immediate surroundings, and adding a wide border to fit their purposes. I've not seen the results, but I know that they are both pleased.

COMPTON PILLOW

CANVAS: 12# to the inch (5# to the cm)

DESIGN AREA: 15 × 21 inches (38 × 53 cm)

STITCH: Tent, with number of threads as below

NEEDLE: Size 18

YARN: Appleton Tapestry, one thread (or Paternayan Persian, in square brackets on chart, 2 strands), for the design

973	[462]	– 2 skeins		205	[872]	– 6 skeins
293	[603]	– 3 skeins		207	[870]	– 2 skeins
294	[601]	– 2 skeins		184	[432]	– 3 skeins
901	} [443]	– { 3 skeins		861	[855]	– 1 skein
762		– { 2 skeins		882	[263]	– 2 skeins
984	[454]	– 2 skeins		703	[494]	– 2 skeins
986	[453]	– 6 skeins		708	[490]	– 3 skeins
691	[444]	– 1 skein		155	[533]	– 1 skein
692	[754]	– 2 skeins		993	[220]	– 4 skeins
204	[485]	– 3 skeins				

Appleton Crewel for the background (four threads)
588 – 14 skeins, 998 – 7 skeins, 298 – 7 skeins
OR Paternayan Persian (2 strands)
220 – 14 skeins, 420 – 14 skeins

Quantities are for the pillow cover using Appleton yarns.

The background is worked with a blend of Appleton yarns: 2 threads of 588, 1 of 998, and 1 of 298 in the needle give the very dark, soft – but not black – hue of the original. If you find that four threads are too bulky for your tension, use just one of each of the three colors in your needle. (One thread of each color of the Paternayan will give a similar effect, but do not expect it to be identical.) The background may be continued for an extra two rows beyond the design. A pure black border (four skeins) could be stitched.

•

*The pillow is an adaptation of one end
of the rug; it is worked on finer canvas, which creates a smaller design.
It complements the rug, of course, but stands equally well on its own –
I particularly like it on the magnificent "Empire" bed.*

COMPTON PILLOW

KEY

207 [870]
205 [872]
204 [485]
861 [855]
708 [490]
703 [494]
882 [263]
691 [444]
692 [754]
901 [443]
986 [453]
984 [454]
762 [443]
184 [432]
973 [462]
155 [533]
293 [603]
294 [601]
993 [220]

Background
588, 298 & 998
[220 & 420]
☆
Middle point

130 140 150 160 170 180 190 200 210 220 230 240 250 260 267

19

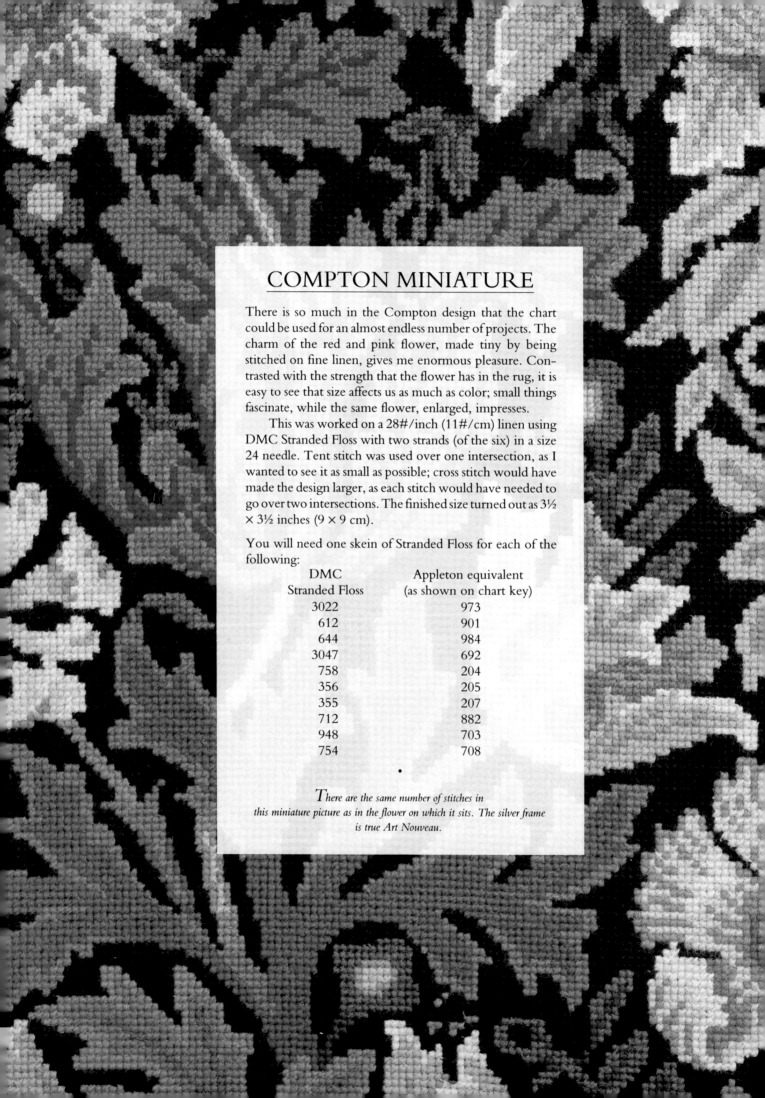

COMPTON MINIATURE

There is so much in the Compton design that the chart could be used for an almost endless number of projects. The charm of the red and pink flower, made tiny by being stitched on fine linen, gives me enormous pleasure. Contrasted with the strength that the flower has in the rug, it is easy to see that size affects us as much as color; small things fascinate, while the same flower, enlarged, impresses.

This was worked on a 28#/inch (11#/cm) linen using DMC Stranded Floss with two strands (of the six) in a size 24 needle. Tent stitch was used over one intersection, as I wanted to see it as small as possible; cross stitch would have made the design larger, as each stitch would have needed to go over two intersections. The finished size turned out as 3½ × 3½ inches (9 × 9 cm).

You will need one skein of Stranded Floss for each of the following:

DMC Stranded Floss	Appleton equivalent (as shown on chart key)
3022	973
612	901
644	984
3047	692
758	204
356	205
355	207
712	882
948	703
754	708

•

There are the same number of stitches in this miniature picture as in the flower on which it sits. The silver frame is true Art Nouveau.

HARE & FOX

IN 1887 WILLIAM MORRIS completed the design for his tapestry "The Forest." It is a remarkable work, probably woven by William Knight at Merton Abbey. Originally bought by Alexander Ionides for his house in London, it is 48 inches (120 cm) high by 177 inches (450 cm) wide and is now in the collection of London's Victoria & Albert Museum.

Morris frequently avoided drawing birds and animals in his early years of designing and more often than not recruited his friend Philip Webb, the architect, to draw them for him. The wonderful swirling forest is typically Morris and gives all the atmosphere of deep woodland. The illogicality of finding not only the fox and hare, but also a lion, a peacock, and a raven in close proximity seems not to matter at all.

The mood of the piece is medieval, and the "mille fleurs" – the flowers in the foreground – add to this. They are reminiscent of the Cluny tapestries of the sixteenth century and are believed to have been drawn partly by Philip Webb with help from Morris's most famous pupil, Henry Dearle. The knowledge that so many people could contribute to one glorious work in such a harmonious way reminds me of Morris's belief in the meaning of creative work and the joy that can be achieved through it.

To attempt to adapt the whole tapestry to one piece of needlepoint is clearly not very practical. Few rooms could accommodate such a large piece, and even the most enthusiastic needleworker might find the project daunting. I decided therefore to start with the Hare and make it pillow-size. It is an obvious choice; the Hare is shown head-on, and the colors are totally naturalistic.

It worked so well that the Fox was voted an essential successor. He needed to be larger than the Hare, and the foliage around him was made more lush by adding an extra shade around the veins of the leaves. I also brightened up the flowers considerably, taking into account that the original probably had faded. The effect is that even though the Fox is in a deeper part of the forest, a ray of sunshine has penetrated to spotlight him and the flowers. The Hare, hiding in the shadows, has seen him.

I found the two pretty chairs a few years ago and had never been able to decide on a design for them. A tracery of small flowers seemed the most suitable solution, but rather too obvious. One day the Hare pillow was sitting on one of the chairs; it looked so completely at home that the decision

•

The Hare and the Fox pillows are taken from William Morris's 1887 tapestry "The Forest." Here they look perfectly at home in their natural habitat in the English countryside.

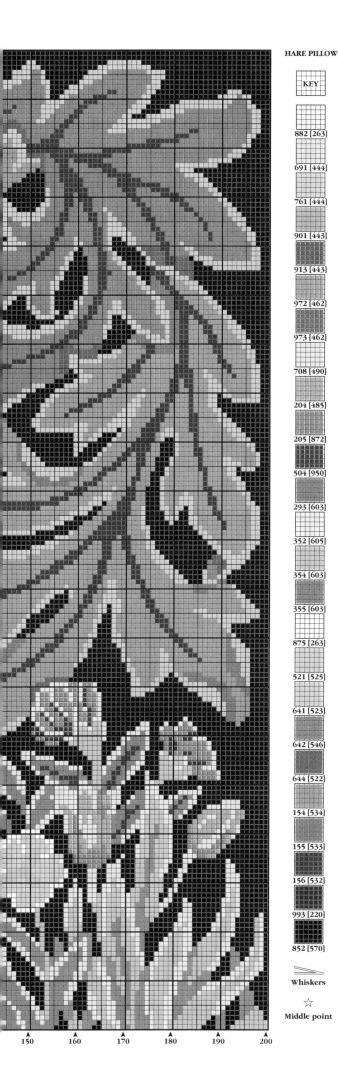

KEY

882 [263]
691 [444]
761 [444]
901 [443]
913 [443]
972 [462]
973 [462]
708 [490]
204 [485]
205 [872]
504 [950]
293 [603]
352 [605]
354 [603]
355 [603]
875 [263]
521 [525]
641 [523]
642 [546]
644 [522]
154 [534]
155 [533]
156 [532]
993 [220]
852 [570]

Whiskers

☆ Middle point

150 160 170 180 190 200

was taken to rework both Hare and Fox to fit. Although the chairs are very small, the designs did not quite cover them. When the template was made, I was able to use my printed kit version to see how much extra design was needed. The foreground had to be extended forward and to the sides – it just meant elongating the leaves and stems and making up or repeating a few on each edge. I considered extending the swirling acanthus leaves, but decided that they were too complicated. For larger chairs (and most are), you could use the chart and work on coarser canvas, although exactly how the design will need to be altered will depend on your chair. With the flowers and foliage growing in a random way, you have a great deal of freedom.

HARE PILLOW

CANVAS: 14# to the inch (5½# to the cm)

DESIGN AREA: 14 × 14 inches (36 × 36 cm)

STITCH: Tent

NEEDLE: Size 20

YARN: Appleton Crewel, 3 threads (or Paternayan Persian, in square brackets on charts, 2 strands)

691	[444]	1 skein	352	[605]	4 skeins
901		1 skein	354		2 skeins
761	[443]	2 skeins	355	[603]	2 skeins
913		1 skein	293		2 skeins
882	[263]	1 skein	156	[532]	4 skeins
972	[462]	3 skeins	155	[533]	2 skeins
973		1 skein	154	[534]	7 skeins
504	[950]	1 skein	521	[525]	3 skeins
708	[490]	1 skein	644	[D522]	1 skein
204	[485]	1 skein	642	[D546]	7 skeins
205	[872]	1 skein	641	[523]	3 skeins
875	[236]	1 skein	993	[220]	1 skein
852	[570]	7 skeins (Background)			

Quantities are for the Hare Pillow worked in Appleton yarns.

The original Hare contains all the colors mentioned, but, in order to move gently from one color to another, some colors were blended together in the needle. No hares, as far as I know, are identical, and the shading of their fur changes as the light falls on it, so you are free to experiment with the shades and create your own unique markings. When the stitching is complete, you can give your Hare some whiskers and eyebrows, using white sewing thread to make long stitches across the surface.

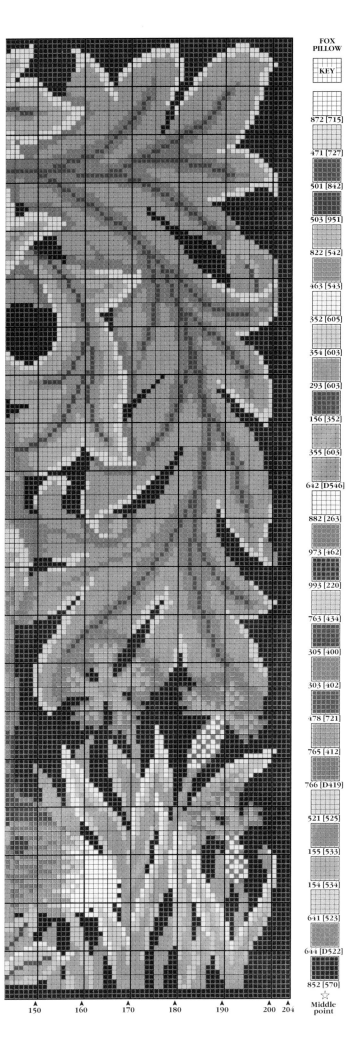

872 [715]
471 [727]
501 [842]
503 [951]
822 [542]
463 [543]
352 [605]
354 [603]
293 [603]
156 [352]
355 [603]
642 [D546]
882 [263]
973 [462]
993 [220]
763 [434]
305 [400]
303 [402]
478 [721]
765 [412]
766 [D419]
521 [525]
155 [533]
154 [534]
641 [523]
644 [D522]
852 [570]
☆
Middle
point

▲ 150 ▲ 160 ▲ 170 ▲ 180 ▲ 190 ▲ 200 204

FOX PILLOW

CANVAS: 14# to the inch (5½# to the cm)

DESIGN AREA: 14 × 14 inches (36 × 36 cm)

STITCH: Tent

NEEDLE: Size 20

YARN: Appleton Crewel, 3 threads (or Paternayan Persian, in square brackets on chart, 2 strands)

872	[715]	– 1 skein	973	[462]	– 1 skein
471	[727]	– 1 skein	993	[220]	– 1 skein
501	[842]	– 1 skein	763	[434]	– 1 skein
503	[951]	– 1 skein	305	[400]	– 1 skein
822	[542]	– 1 skein	303	[402]	– 2 skeins
463	[543]	– 1 skein	478	[721]	– 1 skein
352	[605]	– 2 skeins	765	[412]	– 2 skeins
354		– 2 skeins	766	[D419]	– 2 skeins
293	[603]	– 2 skeins	521	[525]	– 1 skein
355		– 2 skeins	155	[533]	– 4 skeins
156	[532]	– 2 skeins	154	[534]	– 4 skeins
642	[D546]	– 7 skeins	641	[523]	– 2 skeins
882	[263]	– 1 skein	644	[D522]	– 7 skeins
852	[570]	– 11 skeins (Background)			

Quantities are for the pillow cover worked in Appleton yarns.

If you have to add to either design to accommodate a chair seat, or would just like to show more background, you will need more yarn (see page 113).

In nature, the colors in foliage are quite fickle. Sometimes the veins of leaves are dark, sometimes light. As one leaf cuts the light from another, the shadow can cause two quite different shades on the same leaf – and so it is when sunlight strikes. Paint with your yarn and create your own forest.

•

(Previous page)
The Hare and Fox have been adapted to
fit these pretty "spoon-back" chairs and are photographed in the
beautiful library at 8 Addison Road, the house designed by Halsey
Ricardo for Sir Ernest Debenham in 1904. So many details in this
extraordinary house are treats for the enthusiast of fine workmanship.
It is now owned by The Richmond Fellowship.

WOODPECKER

THIS WAS THE FIRST of William Morris's own designs for a tapestry. The tapestry was woven at Merton Abbey in about 1885, and the original is now at the William Morris Gallery in Walthamstow, London. As you can see, it is much longer than my version and included a honeysuckle border and a piece from a poem by Morris referring to an Italian legend where a king is turned into a woodpecker.

I once a king and chief, now am the tree bark's thief;
ever twixt trunk and leaf, chasing the prey.

The sizes of canvas available and the practicality of showing a finished piece in a modern home sometimes – regrettably

– force me to adapt a design. On this occasion, I have omitted the border and shortened the whole design to make it a sensible size for a fire screen. The canvas, 14 threads to

the inch, allowed as much detail as was needed for this size.

The wealth of design and almost total lack of plain background reminded me once again of Frank Brangwyn; the swirling acanthus leaves almost move – in total contrast to the very still and watchful birds.

WOODPECKER

CANVAS: 14# to the inch (5½# to the cm)

DESIGN AREA: 23 × 16 inches (58 × 41 cm)

STITCH: Tent

NEEDLE: Size 20

YARN: Appleton Crewel, 3 threads (or Paternayan Persian, in square brackets on chart, 2 strands)

352	[605]	– 7 skeins	641	[523]	– 4 skeins
354		– 7 skeins	477	[722]	– 2 skeins
355	[603]	– 7 skeins	474	[725]	– 4 skeins
293		– 7 skeins	472	[703]	– 2 skeins
294	[601]	– 4 skeins	471	[727]	– 2 skeins
156	[532]	– 2 skeins	841	[704]	– 1 skein
155	[533]	– 7 skeins	692	[754]	– 2 skeins
154	[534]	– 7 skeins	913	[433]	– 1 skein
521	[525]	– 7 skeins	902	[442]	– 4 skeins
873	[615]	– 2 skeins	762	[443]	– 2 skeins
874	[624]	– 2 skeins	206	[871]	– 1 skein
644	[D522]	– 4 skeins	993	[220]	– 1 skein
642	[D546]	– 7 skeins	504	[950]	– 1 skein
852	[570]	– 11 skeins (Background)			

These are quantities for Woodpecker worked in Appleton yarns.

Should you want to increase the size to fit a particular piece of furniture, but do not wish to change the canvas gauge, the design could be continued in the appropriate direction. For instance, the half orange at the top right could be completed; use one of the other oranges as a color guide. The branches could be elongated and the leaves completed. Another alternative would be to stitch a "frame" of appropriate width in stripes of two or more colors.

•

The original Woodpecker tapestry, with its poem, swirling acanthus leaves, and honeysuckle border, is a most beautiful design. Woven in 1885, it is now in the collection of the William Morris Gallery in Walthamstow.
My version, photographed with a miniature orange tree, is perhaps a more practical size for the home of today.

In addition to this handsome picture, the Woodpecker would also make a marvelous fire screen. At nearly 10 feet, Morris's original tapestry is even longer than the Honeysuckle bellpull. The two stitched models blend well together in a room, as one would expect. Although bellpulls are rarely used nowadays for their original purpose, they serve as very pretty decorations.

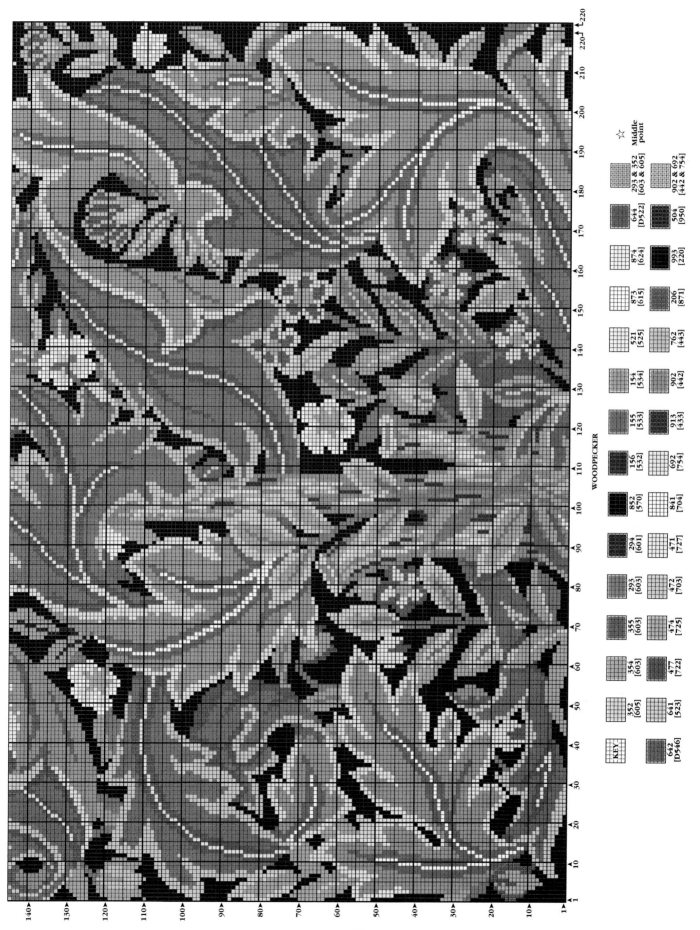

WOODPECKER

KEY

642 [D546]	641 [523]	477 [722]	474 [725]
352 [605]	354 [603]	355 [603]	293 [603]
294 [601]	852 [570]	156 [532]	155 [533]
154 [534]	521 [525]	873 [615]	874 [624]
644 [D522]	293 & 352 [603 & 605]		

472 [703]	471 [727]
841 [704]	692 [754]
913 [433]	902 [442]
762 [443]	206 [871]
993 [220]	504 [950]
902 & 692 [442 & 754]	☆ Middle point

HONEYSUCKLE

THE HONEYSUCKLE BORDER to William Morris's Wood-pecker tapestry is too good to be lost altogether, so here it is as a bellpull. Honeysuckle recurs frequently in Morris's designs, but I found reproducing the very thin petals on canvas a little daunting.

The proportions are closer to Morris's original than those of my shortened version of Woodpecker. As I have explained, the central panel would be too large for most houses (and stitchers!) if it were made to its original height. The length of Honeysuckle is, however, perfectly reasonable for a bellpull.

I am always eager to explore all the possibilities of a design. If Honeysuckle were stitched on 28#/inch (11#/cm) linen over one thread, for instance, the length should fit the depth of the shortened Woodpecker. It would measure 3 × 23 inches (7.5 × 58 cm). However, I hesitate to recommend doing this without first trying it myself. It would be necessary to make a feature of the differences in the gauge and weight of the backing fabric, perhaps by working Honeysuckle in stranded floss on dark linen. Then what could be done with the area above and below the Woodpecker? Maybe the Honeysuckle design could be adapted even more to fit across. Morris "cheated" by covering those areas with his scroll and poem. New ideas tumble in. This really is where my pleasure comes from . . . the challenge . . . the involvement . . . the slight uncertainty . . . and the joy when it all goes well.

HONEYSUCKLE BELLPULL

CANVAS: 14# to the inch (5½# to the cm)

DESIGN AREA: 48½ × 6 inches (123 × 15 cm)

STITCH: Tent

NEEDLE: Size 20

YARN: Appleton Crewel, 3 threads (or Paternayan Persian, in square brackets on charts, 2 strands)

692	[754]	– 7 skeins	861	[855]	– 2 skeins
902	[442]	– 4 skeins	352	[605]	– 9 skeins
762	[443]	– 1 skein	354		– 9 skeins
913	[433]	– 14 skeins	355	[603]	– 3 skeins
703	[494]	– 2 skeins	293		– 3 skeins
708	[490]	– 2 skeins	294	[601]	– 3 skeins
204	[485]	– 2 skeins	877	[948]	– 1 skein
926	[511]	– 7 skeins (Background)			

Quantities are for the bellpull using Appleton.

The Honeysuckle bellpull welcomes us to the magnificent Stanmore Hall in Middlesex, England. Built between 1837 and 1850, it was purchased in 1888 by William Knox D'Arcy, who commissioned William Morris to provide the internal decoration and fittings, Edward Burne-Jones for lavish tapestries, and William Lethaby to assist with stonework and fittings in conjunction with Morris.

HONEYSUCKLE
BELL PULL

KEY

692 [754]

913 [433]

902 [442]

762 [443]

352 [605]

354 [603]

355 [603]

293 [603]

294 [601]

877 [948]

703 [494]

708 [490]

861 [855]

204 [485]

926 [511]

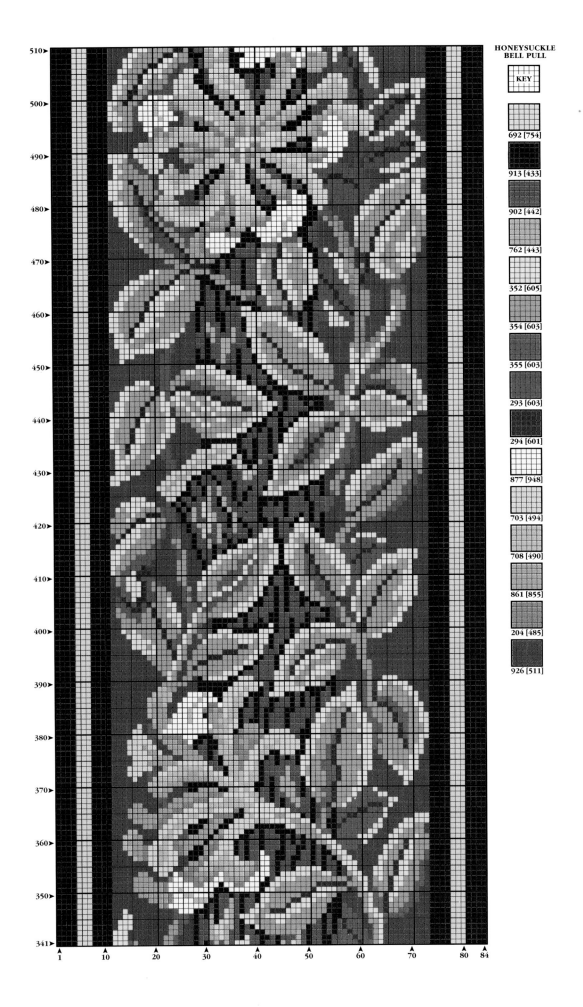

KEY

692 [754]

913 [433]

902 [442]

762 [443]

352 [605]

354 [603]

355 [603]

293 [603]

294 [601]

877 [948]

703 [494]

708 [490]

861 [855]

204 [485]

926 [511]

FLOWERPOT

MORRIS & COMPANY started to produce embroidery kits in 1878. They could be bought with the outline drawn or printed on the fabric, or the design could be placed on the customer's own material. These pieces were meant as pillows or small panels. If desired, they could be completed by the embroideresses at Morris & Company. Although this latter activity would have brought income to Morris's firm, he preferred that the end user should also be involved in and enjoy the work leading up to its realization.

Flowerpot is one of the earliest examples of a Morris & Company kit. In her excellent book *William Morris Textiles*, Linda Parry notes that in 1875 Morris would have seen a new acquisition at the Victoria & Albert Museum: two seventeenth-century Italian designs, from which he almost certainly drew inspiration for his Flowerpot. I know of two worked samples. The one in the Victoria & Albert Museum is an embroidered piece worked in chain stitch and French knots on wool flannel. The piece that can be seen at the William Morris Gallery at Walthamstow was stitched on

May Morris's original Flowerpot embroidery, in the collection of the William Morris Gallery.

•

This fairy-tale cottage, which houses more conventional flowerpots, is a perfect setting for the completed pillow. Although Morris's Flowerpot has an Eastern feel, it blends well with the gray of the wicker chair and the rambling twigs of the wintery English countryside.

linen by Morris's daughter, May, using silks and gold thread worked in satin stitch, long and short, stem stitch, and running stitch, as well as chain stitch and French knots.

For me, Flowerpot has an Eastern look not apparent in similar subsequent designs for Morris kits – the Persian-style vase, the improbable symmetry of the stylized flowers and their beautiful curving stems. My version is worked on canvas using tent stitch; and, of course, the whole canvas is covered, not just the outlines. The colors remain close to the original May Morris version.

The chart allows you to extract a section for a smaller project; just one flower worked on the same gauge of canvas makes a dainty pincushion.

FLOWERPOT PILLOW

CANVAS: 14# to the inch (5½# to the cm)

DESIGN AREA: 15½ × 15 inches (39 × 38 cm)

STITCH: Tent

NEEDLE: Size 20

YARN: Appleton Crewel, 3 threads (or Paternayan Persian, in square brackets on chart, 2 strands)

873	[615]	– 1 skein	226	[D211]	– 1 skein
874	[624]	– 7 skeins	128	[920]	– 1 skein
353	[604]	– 4 skeins	877	[948]	– 5 skeins
354	[603]	– 4 skeins	708	[490]	– 4 skeins
355		– 4 skeins	204	[485]	– 1 skein
221	[490]	– 1 skein	761	[444]	– 3 skeins
222	[933]	– 2 skeins	762	[443]	– 5 skeins
223	[D275]	– 1 skein	875	[236]	– 14 skeins
224	[D234]	– 1 skein			

Quantities are for the pillow cover worked in Appleton yarns.

•

(Overleaf)
For many years, I have admired May Morris's embroidered original, so it seems appropriate that my interpretation should be seen on a frame once used by May herself. One of her co-embroiderers in Hammersmith was Fanny Becket, and Fanny's son-in-law, John Masterson, kindly let me use the frame – much to my delight. The pincushion shows one of the flowers stitched on finer canvas in slightly darker coral colors.

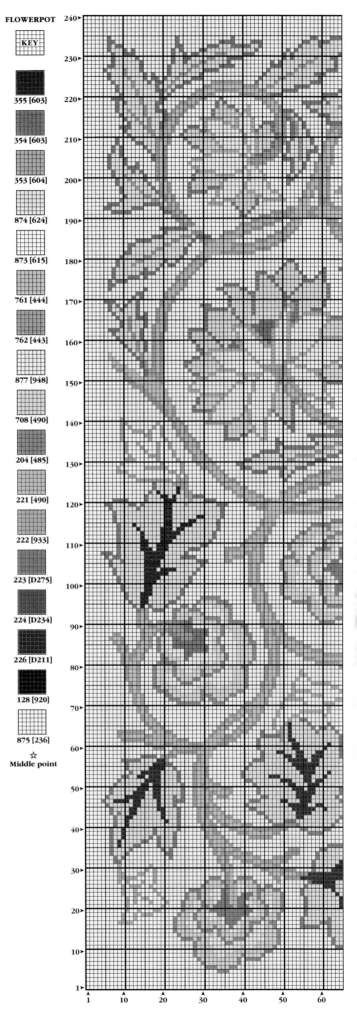

FLOWERPOT

KEY

355 [603]
354 [603]
353 [604]
874 [624]
873 [615]
761 [444]
762 [443]
877 [948]
708 [490]
204 [485]
221 [490]
222 [933]
223 [D275]
224 [D234]
226 [D211]
128 [920]
875 [236]
☆ Middle point

JACKFIELD ROSE

A GREAT DEAL of the Ironbridge Gorge, in Shropshire, England, has been turned into a fascinating re-creation of industrial manufacturing in the 1800s. One of the most important industries in the area was ceramic tile-making.

In the 1860s and 1870s, the influence of some of our greatest designers – William Morris, William De Morgan, Edward Burne-Jones, and Walter Crane – caused a revolution in tile design similar to those which they were creating in textile design, painting, and illustration. The Jackfield Tile Museum at Ironbridge has a superb display of many of the better tiles from this period. My visit there was all too short, but my memory of a washstand with a tiled back is most vivid. It features a group of tiles, each showing a different flower which spills over its borders. There was such a lot of design in so small an area that I wanted to see the flowers individually, so that they could not detract from each other. Here is the Rose, with its geometric border.

I have adapted it slightly: there are only two roses on the small tile, but the larger format left rather a lot of background to stitch, so another flower has been added. The background was originally a very deep blue, which you might like to try. I see the "tile" not just as a pillow or picture, but possibly inset on the front of a chest or pretty door – or as a workbox or table top.

You can see that just part of the design can also be used to decorate a tablecloth, and the theme could be continued by stitching a single rosebud on each napkin. A tray cloth might have a small sprig of a rose, a twig, and a few leaves. With the chart you are free to choose how little or how much you wish to show.

My inspiration for this embroidery came from the beautiful tiles on this Victorian washstand at the Jackfield Tile Museum, in Ironbridge. As you can see, there are many others here to inspire!
My first version was intended as a picture and has been mounted on a board ready for framing.

•

A part of the design has been transferred to the corner of a tablecloth. The photograph below shows how we marked its position with basting stitches.
(Overleaf) The design on the white linen tablecloth contrasts interestingly with the heavier wool version, now made into a pillow.

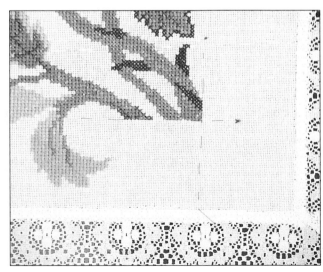

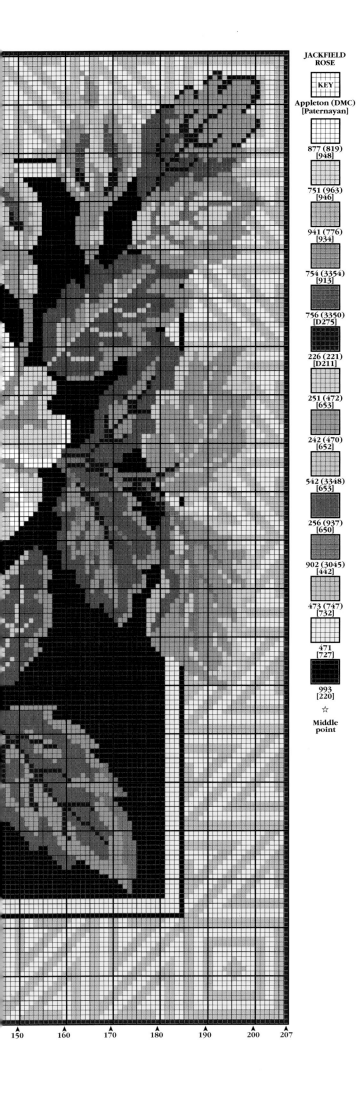

JACKFIELD ROSE

KEY

Appleton (DMC) [Paternayan]

877 (819) [948]

751 (963) [946]

941 (776) [934]

754 (3354) [913]

756 (3350) [D275]

226 (221) [D211]

251 (472) [653]

242 (470) [652]

542 (3348) [653]

256 (937) [650]

902 (3045) [442]

473 (747) [732]

471 [727]

993 [220]

☆ Middle point

JACKFIELD ROSE

PILLOW/PICTURE

CANVAS: 14# to the inch (5½# to the cm)

DESIGN AREA: 14½ × 14½ inches (37 × 37 cm)

STITCH: Tent

NEEDLE: Size 20

YARN: Appleton Crewel, 3 threads (or Paternayan Persian, in square brackets on chart, 2 strands)

877	[948]	– 2 skeins	242	[652]	– 5 skeins
751	[946]	– 4 skeins	256	[650]	– 4 skeins
941	[934]	– 2 skeins	902	[442]	– 2 skeins
754	[913]	– 4 skeins	471	[727]	– 7 skeins
756	[D275]	– 1 skein	473	[732]	– 7 skeins
226	[D211]	– 2 skeins	993	[220]	– 7 skeins

251 ⎫ [653] – ⎰ 2 skeins
542 ⎭ – ⎱ 1 skein

Quantities are for the pillow/picture using Appleton yarns.

TABLECLOTH

LINEN: 28# to the inch (11# to the cm)

DESIGN AREA: 9½ × 9½ inches (24 × 24 cm)

STITCH: Cross, with 2 threads of the six-stranded floss

NEEDLE: Size 24

THREAD: DMC Stranded Floss (in brackets on the chart)

819 – 1 skein	472 – 1 skein
963 – 2 skeins	3348 – 1 skein
776 – 1 skein	470 – 1 skein
3354 – 1 skein	937 – 1 skein
3350 – 1 skein	3045 – 1 skein
221 – 1 skein	744 – 1 skein

These are quantities for the tablecloth shown.

As the cross stitch on the 28# linen tablecloth is worked over two threads, the design remains exactly the same size as on the 14# canvas. It was an ideal choice for the corner of a cloth, as the stem emerges from the corner of the picture. The effect would have been crowded if it had touched the lace, so 51 linen threads were counted off and marked with a basting thread to form the inside corner; the basting is, of course, removed after the design is finished. I have to confess that to make life easy I bought the lace-trimmed tablecloth. It measures 54 inches (137 cm) square. For a smaller cloth, I would advise using a smaller part of the design or working this larger part over one thread only (tent stitch would be safer – see page 118).

AFRICAN MARIGOLD

THE WILLIAM MORRIS Gallery in Walthamstow, London, houses, among other lovely things, the original watercolor for this Morris design. I was immediately attracted by its unfinished "working drawing" quality and by the extremely delicate blues. Unlike Pomegranate (page 66), African Marigold did achieve maturity and is still being produced by Liberty of London as a curtain and furnishing fabric. The colors in the Liberty versions are simpler than those in the watercolor, but the company makes several interesting alternative color combinations that show very clearly how different a design can look when colors are changed. However, the sweeping, swirling movement of the leaves is, whatever the coloring, unmistakably Morris.

There are two parts to this design; I chose the large main flower as the center of my adaptation. The blue leaves that ribbon around the large flower required very careful shading to keep the blue true to the original and to retain the movement and depth. The large flower, with its very soft coloring, was no easier. You can shade subtly from white to blue or light yellow with watercolors, but producing the same delicacy in solid-colored yarn and pre-ordained stitch shapes is quite a challenge. Several "roughs"

were stitched for this design. In the Liberty version, the marigolds are shown in a light orange, but I preferred to retain the faded look of the original watercolor.

It would be most enjoyable, and another challenge, to make a partner with one of the smaller flowers as the focal point. The complete design would also make a lovely rug, and I have promised myself to undertake that one day, increasing the gauge of the canvas and producing a series of squares which could be stitched together and surrounded with an attractive border. Or, on much finer canvas, one of the smaller marigolds would make a very pretty pincushion or potpourri sachet.

•

The delicate watercolor shows Morris's first interpretation of the design and the one I fell in love with; it can be seen at the William Morris Gallery, Walthamstow. "Tom Tit," the cat, seems more interested in African Marigolds than snowdrops! (Overleaf) The colors of the pillow blend perfectly with the soft pine and a marvelous collection of blue and white transferware china.

AFRICAN MARIGOLD

CANVAS: 12# to the inch (5# to the cm)

DESIGN AREA: 15½ × 15½ inches (39 × 39 cm)

STITCH: Tent

NEEDLE: Size 18

YARN: Appleton Tapestry, 1 thread (or Paternayan Persian, 2 strands, in square brackets on chart)

691	[444]	– 2 skeins	321		– 6 skeins
692	[754]	– 1 skein	322	[513]	– 1 skein
693	[734]	– 1 skein	324	[512]	– 3 skeins
901	[443]	– 1 skein	325	[511]	– 2 skeins
876	[213]	– 2 skeins	352	[605]	– 4 skeins
521	[525]	– 4 skeins	293	[603]	– 2 skeins
641	[523]	– 2 skeins	992	[263]	– 9 skeins

Quantities are for the pillow cover using Appleton yarns.

If you have to add to the design, or would just like to show more background, you will need more yarn (see page 113).

58

AFRICAN
MARIGOLD

KEY

691 [444]

692 [754]

693 [734]

901 [443]

876 [213]

521 [525]

641 [523]

321 [513]

322 [513]

324 [512]

325 [511]

352 [605]

293 [603]

992 [263]

**Middle
point**

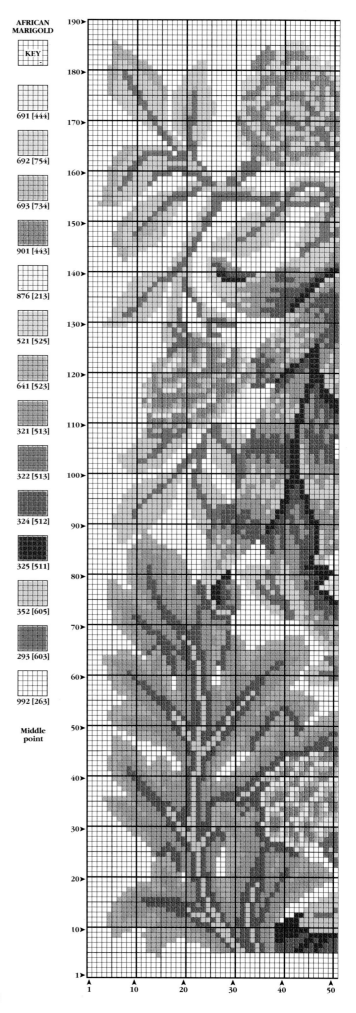

JASMINE

JASMINE TRAIL is one of Morris's earliest known fabric designs; its light, delicate, and meandering stems, flowers, and leaves make it a perfect subject for a repeating pattern. Here is just a section with no repeats; the plant shapes allow me the freedom to stop and leave a space for an initial without appearing unnatural.

My original interpretation fitted the top of a small workbox, for which no background stitching was necessary, as the pale yellow of the fine canvas provided a suitable shade. Naturally, great care had to be taken to avoid carrying the threads across a blank area at the back of the work.

It was worked again as a tiny pillow, which could also double as a container for sweet-smelling herbs (or something scented with jasmine).

I tried it a third time with pink-edged flowers instead of the original colors. In this version (from the same chart), the flowers and leaves are stitched in stranded floss to give them a sheen. The trellis is worked in wool yarn, using a line of backstitch on each side of the tent stitch to imitate the grain of the wood. The border of this version is the invention of Angela Kahan; it gives a lovely lacy effect. The center of the diamonds are over eight canvas threads, reducing down to two. The corners are mitered.

Increasing the size of this design by working on a coarser gauge of canvas did not appeal to me as I like the delicacy of the flowers. There are numerous ways to increase the size of a pillow; the worked piece can be attached to a ready-made larger pillow, or you can add a ruffle or a lace edging. It really depends on which version has been stitched, where it is intended to rest, and your personal preference.

JASMINE

CANVAS: 17# to the inch (7# to the cm)

DESIGN AREA: 8½ × 8½ inches (22 × 22 cm)
9½ × 9½ inches (24 × 24 cm) with border

NEEDLE: Size 22

YELLOW FLOWER VERSION (1st colorway)

STITCH: Tent
YARN: Appleton Crewel, 2 threads (or Paternayan Persian, n square brackets on chart, 1 strand)

991b	[260]	– 1 skein	547	[691]	– 2 skeins
844	[714]	– 1 skein	901	[443]	– 1 skein
551	[773]	– 1 skein	765	[412]	– 1 skein
255	[651]	– 2 skeins			

Pillow background: 882 [756] – 7 skeins

PINK FLOWER VERSION (2nd colorway)

STITCH: Tent and backstitch, with one thread (six strands) of floss or two threads of yarn

YARN: DMC Stranded Floss, in round brackets

Blanc	– 1 skein	581	– 3 skeins
963	– 1 skein	937	– 3 skeins
819	– 1 skein		
761	– 1 skein (Appleton Crewel Wool)		
764	– 1 skein (Appleton Crewel Wool)		

Background: 875 – 7 skeins (Appleton Crewel Wool)

To position your chosen initial, find the center of the relevant space on the canvas (after completing the design and *before* stitching the background) and mark with a knot. On the charts, the optical center of each initial is marked ★. Count from there, using the two shades of Appleton green (255 and 547) or DMC (581 and 937).

If the background is not going to be stitched, it is essential that the threads do not run across unworked parts of the canvas, as they will show through. Note that both of the yellow flower versions are worked entirely in tent stitch. For the pink flower version, the trellis has been stitched with a central row of tent stitch and the two outside rows in backstitch (see below). This arrangement takes up less space than the three rows of tent stitch on the chart. You will need to adjust the leaves where they pass under the trellis – a few extra stitches may be needed to make this convincing. The border can be stitched all in tent stitch if you wish.

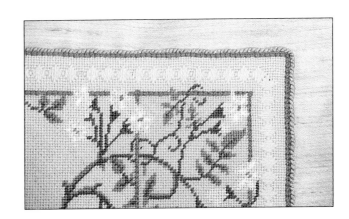

(Opposite)
My latest version of Jasmine – the plant shows how accurate Morris's drawing is. On pages 64/65, the first Jasmine is shown as a box lid and as a tiny pillow. It seems appropriate that they are all shown in sunshine.

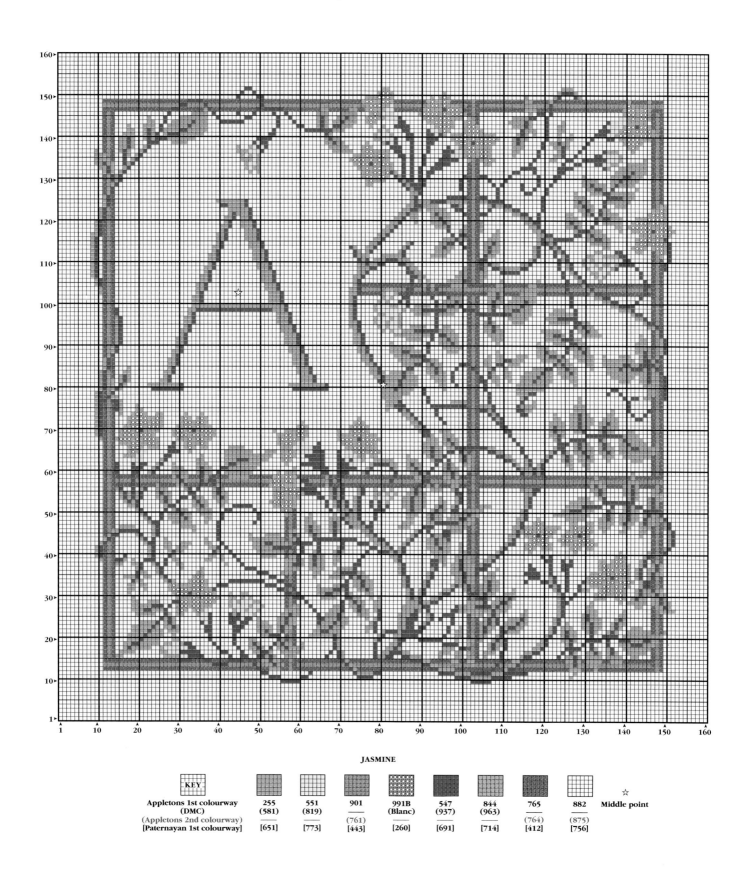

JASMINE

KEY									
Appletons 1st colourway **(DMC)**	**255** **(581)**	**551** **(819)**	**901**	**991B** **(Blanc)**	**547** **(937)**	**844** **(963)**	**765**	**882**	☆
(Appletons 2nd colourway)	—	—	(761)	—	—	—	(764)	(875)	**Middle point**
[Paternayan 1st colourway]	[651]	[773]	[443]	[260]	[691]	[714]	[412]	[756]	

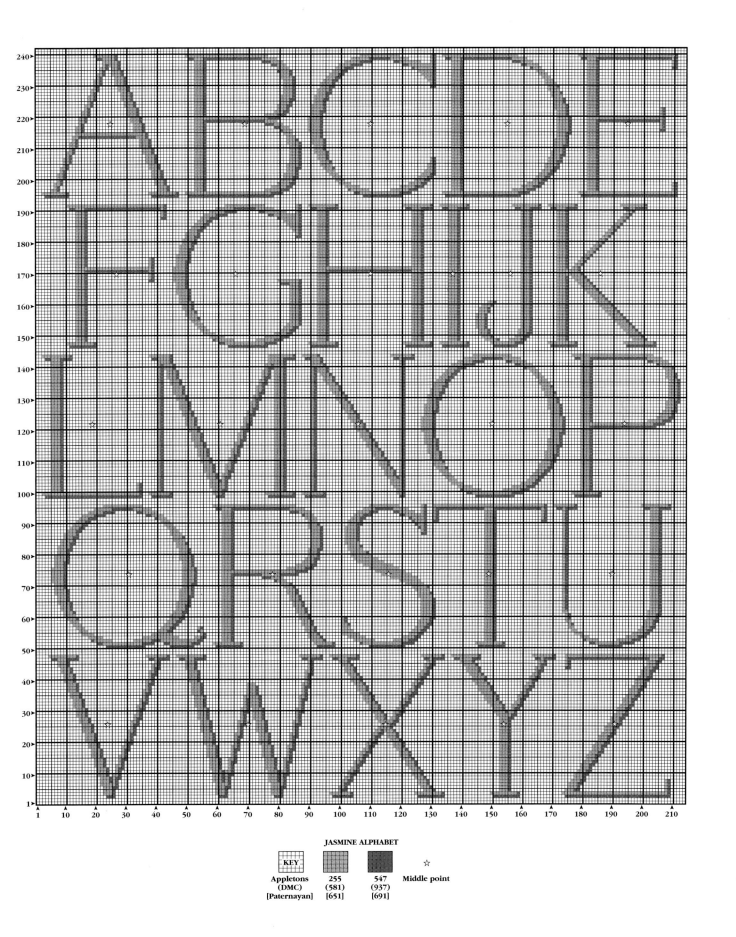

JASMINE ALPHABET

KEY		☆
Appletons (DMC) [Paternayan]	255 (581) [651]	547 (937) [691]	Middle point

POMEGRANATE

T̲HIS RUG̲ is based on an unfinished pencil, ink, and watercolor painting attributed to Morris some time between 1880–1896 and never, to my knowledge, previously completed as a worked piece. The original painting is in the collection of the Victoria & Albert Museum.

As always, I was first attracted by the "unfinished" look of the Morris painting and willingly took up the challenge of completing it. While retaining his original colors, I hope that at the same time I have achieved (humbly!) something

that perhaps even William Morris himself never did. Fortunately, the perfect symmetry of the design made completion comparatively simple without any alteration.

Particularly attractive – and unusual – is the variety of background colors. The lovely curves, so typical of this period, are used as a means to separate the different areas. The intricate central area is perfectly complemented by the gentle simplicity of the border.

At the beginning, I was a little disturbed by the fruit

shapes being dark brown – not an attractive color for fruit, especially as they resemble pineapples and strawberries. However, I felt that any changes would perhaps lose Morris's creative vision and destroy the balance of the design.

Morris does not seem to have given a name to this piece of work, so I invented one. "Pineapples" and "Strawberries" were discounted, and since the center of the design reminded me of the seeds of pomegranates, it became

(Far left) The original Morris watercolor, which inspired my rug.

•

(Above) This fabulous mosaic covers the floor of the main reception room in Stanmore Hall. It was exciting to see it for the first time – no one had told me of its existence. The room is very large, hence the proportionately large design. The leaves, shapes, and flowing stems are so typically Morris that just placing Pomegranate on the stones was enough – the photograph was complete.

67

"Pomegranate." There are other Morris designs with this title, but it seems the most appropriate name.

While the shapes are relatively simple, this is the most difficult of all the designs to adapt by using the chart in a different way. A new color scheme would take a considerable time to work out; the background to each section would need to be stitched as well as the foreground shapes. It also proved difficult to extract a part of the design; the center does not work very well as a pillow. The whole central panel, however, would work as a piano stool top stitched on finer canvas; you would need to calculate carefully and increase the border if necessary.

POMEGRANATE RUG

CANVAS: 8# to the inch (3# to the cm)

DESIGN AREA: 25 × 50 inches (64 × 127 cm)

STITCH: Cross

NEEDLE: Size 16

YARN: Appleton Tapestry, 1 thread (or Paternayan Persian, 2 strands, in square brackets on chart)

764	[413]	– 30 skeins	542	[653]	– 24 skeins
761	[444]	– 3 skeins	873	[615]	– 6 skeins
588	[420]	– 33 skeins	882	[263]	– 3 skeins
185	[431]	– 1 skein	128	[920]	– 2 skeins
184	[432]	– 3 skeins	125	[482]	– 2 skeins
201	[463]	– 2 skeins	202	[406]	– 2 skeins
153	[D389]	– 15 skeins	297	[660]	– 6 skeins
521	[525]	– 12 skeins	692	[754]	– 9 skeins
875	[236]	– 9 skeins	355	[603]	– 3 skeins
356	[601]	– 12 skeins	325	[511]	– 12 skeins

Quantities are for the rug using Appleton yarns.

If you would like to fringe the rug, you will need to buy cord, or you can use yarn (see page 122).

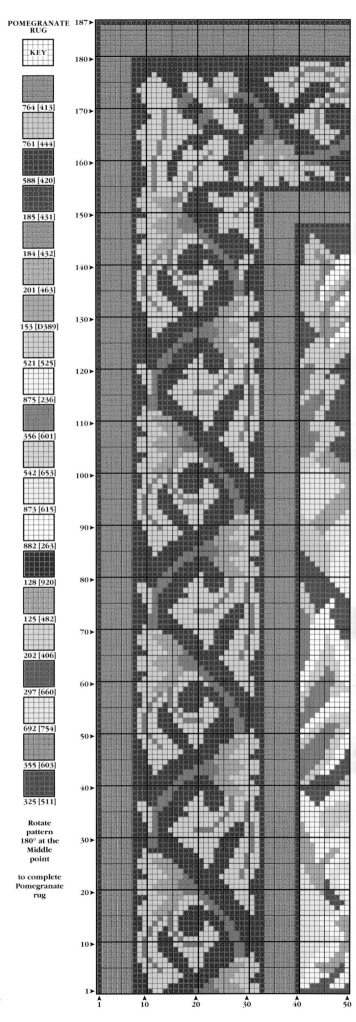

POMEGRANATE RUG

KEY

764 [413]

761 [444]

588 [420]

185 [431]

184 [432]

201 [463]

153 [D389]

521 [525]

875 [236]

356 [601]

542 [653]

873 [615]

882 [263]

128 [920]

125 [482]

202 [406]

297 [660]

692 [754]

355 [603]

325 [511]

Rotate
pattern
180° at the
Middle
point

to complete
Pomegranate
rug

60   70   80   90   100   110   120   130   140   150   160   170   180 185

MORRIS

SOME YEARS AGO, I was allowed to trace this outline, which is attributed to Morris. There was no name for it and no colorings.

The idea of a square rug made from such a strong and elegant design appealed to me. I spent much time stitching different color combinations and finally settled on brown for the background, as it was a color not used much in my Designers Forum collection, and we felt it might harmonize with the decor of a wider range of homes.

Since then, I have hankered after some of the other color schemes that were considered at the time. Preparing this book seemed an ideal excuse to try out some other colors and also provided a practical lesson illustrating the versatility of charts. The rug is on 8#/inch (3#/cm) canvas and measures 42 inches (107 cm) square. The pillows are on 18#/inch (7#/cm) canvas and will measure 18½ inches (46 cm) square. The number of rows on the outside edge has been reduced.

The two partially worked pillows are an opportunity to see the effect that colors have on each other. The shapes in the charts have been adhered to strictly; sometimes the arrangement as well as the choice of the colors has been altered. Very often changing colors alters the balance, and there is a need for more or less weight in a certain part of the design. Three of the four pinks are the same in each pillow, and the darkest of the greens – the fronds in the corner of the center panels – is exactly the same in each. The dark blue version has had the yellows softened from those used in the brown rug.

The background in the center of the light gray pillow has, however, reduced the palest of the green fronds to a soft impression of a design, and the tips of the light blue "petals" are rather lost. If the backgrounds were reversed, the medium green could be used in the border (as in the brown version), but the very palest pink in the center would need to be strengthened.

Given time and patience, using charts is fascinating. If you remove the worry of whether or not the design works as a shape, all your concentration can be directed at experimenting with colors.

•

On the landing at Stanmore Hall. The shape of the ceiling is repeated in the window and in the balustrade, and slightly echoed in the rug. Stanmore Hall was one of the largest commissions for Morris & Company and the most significant just before William Morris's death. Sadly, a fire destroyed some of the interior, but much of the stone and wood work has been painstakingly replaced and returned to its former glory. The Burne-Jones tapestries survived and are now in a private collection.

MORRIS

RUG

CANVAS: 8# to the inch (3# to the cm)

DESIGN AREA: 42 × 42 inches (107 × 107 cm)

STITCH: Cross

NEEDLE: Size 16

YARN: Appleton Tapestry, 1 thread (or Paternayan Persian, 2 strands, in square brackets on chart)

842	[734]	– 15 skeins	293	[603]	– 21 skeins
872	[715]	– 6 skeins	877	[948]	– 6 skeins
762	[443]	– 15 skeins	202	[406]	– 12 skeins
251	[653]	– 33 skeins	204	[485]	– 12 skeins
242	[652]	– 33 skeins	207	[870]	– 6 skeins
128	[920]	– 33 skeins (Background to border)			
585	[421]	– 72 skeins (Background to central panel)			

Quantities are for the rug using Appleton yarns.

PILLOWS

CANVAS: 18# to the inch (7# to the cm)

DESIGN AREA: 18¼ × 18¼ inches (46 × 46 cm)

STITCH: Tent

NEEDLE: Size 22

YARN: Appleton Crewel, 2 threads (or Paternayan Persian, 1 strand, in square brackets on chart)

BLUE PILLOW:	GRAY PILLOW:	
692 [754]	154 [534]	4 skeins
841 [704]	521 [525]	2 skeins
128 [920]	964 [201]	4 skeins
351 [605]	352 [605]	9 skeins
342 [643]	354 ⎱[603]	⎰4 skeins
293 [603]	293 ⎰	⎱6 skeins
704 [493]	181 [475]	2 skeins
202 [406]	202 [406]	4 skeins
204 [485]	204 [485]	4 skeins
124 [484]	124 [484]	2 skeins
929 [510]	989 [246]	9 skeins
326 [511]	151 [203]	16 skeins

Quantities are for the finished pillows worked in Appleton yarns.

•

Partially stitched pillows, using the Morris rug design and changing the gauge of canvas and some of the colors. They provide a fascinating example of how the background color can affect the design colors; the pinks in the border and green in the fronds are the same in each pillow.

Although they appear to be identical, the "squares" of the canvas vary fractionally in each direction; i.e., the distance covered by, say, 200 stitches across the width is slightly different from that covered by 200 stitches along the length. This is caused by the method of production. I also had to make small changes to the exact symmetry of the original drawing to make it "fit." Caution is therefore essential when following the chart to guarantee that you make allowances for these discrepancies. The corner of the chart shown can be copied exactly for its *diagonally opposite* corner, but the *adjacent* corners are "mirror" images of each other, according to which direction you are working.

74

Rotate pattern 180° at middle point to complete Morris Rug.

160 170 180 190 200 210 220 230 240 250 260 270 280 290 300 311

MORRIS RUG

KEY	842 [734]	872 [715]	762 [443]	251 [653]	242 [652]	293 [603]

877 [948]	202 [406]	204 [485]	207 [870]	128 [920]	585 [421]	☆ Middle point

75

KAZAK

WILLIAM MORRIS was a collector of Eastern rugs; he used them for wall hangings, not for the floor. His connection with the designs of the East has been discussed at the beginning of this book, so it seems natural to include an example.

This design would have been contemporary with Morris and his colleagues. The name *Kazak* means that it originated from the Caucasus, and the original might well have been worked by nomadic tribesmen as they traveled on horseback between the Caspian Sea and the Black Sea. Many of the Kazak shapes represented insects such as tarantulas; the nomads included them in order to conquer their fear of them. The zigzag border is also typical of such rugs. The design has none of the flowing shapes we associate with Morris; it has instead the angular look that featured a little later in the Art Deco period. It makes, however, an excellently balanced and well-proportioned rug which I feel would have been admired by contemporary designers, and it fits comfortably with the European designs of the late nineteenth and early twentieth centuries. As with most Eastern rugs, the original from which my Kazak was taken was not quite symmetrical. Muslim beliefs dictate that "only Allah is perfect," and deliberate mistakes are woven in, but I have straightened out all the differences to reduce confusion.

Although the bold colors contrast with most of the other colors in this book, they were all made from natural dyes (such as madder for the warm reds) which, of course, is what Morris himself advocated.

To illustrate the versatility of charts, we also made a bag – a carpet bag, in fact. The rug border is omitted, the gauge of canvas reduced, and the arrangement of the central design adjusted so that the flap of the bag echoes the design beneath it. One of my customers, who wanted something more capacious, stitched a bag using canvas the same gauge as the rug. I had brightened the bag colors a little, but she kept to those of the rug, thus retaining more of a true carpet-bag look.

•

This really dramatic setting is perfect for the Kazak rug. It is seen at 8 Addison Road, London, in the entrance hall with its wonderful gallery on three sides. The mosaic depicts members of the Debenham family and was executed by two Italian brothers. The deep blue tiles and decorated frieze behind are all by De Morgan. The outside of this imposing house is tiled in blue at the top to reflect the sky and green at the bottom to echo the trees.

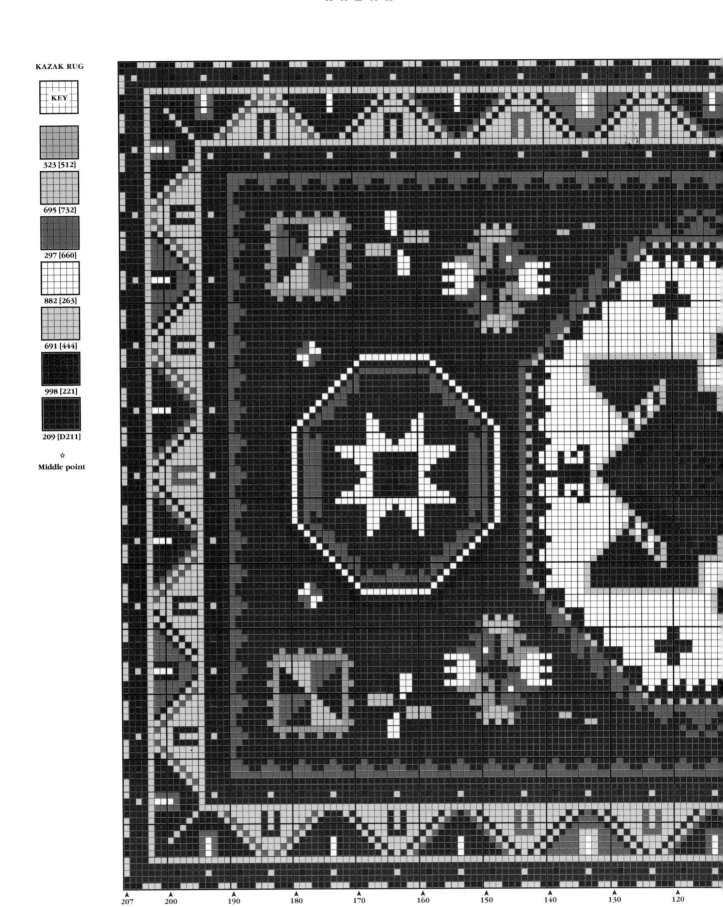

KAZAK RUG

KEY

323 [512]

695 [732]

297 [660]

882 [263]

691 [444]

998 [221]

209 [D211]

☆
Middle point

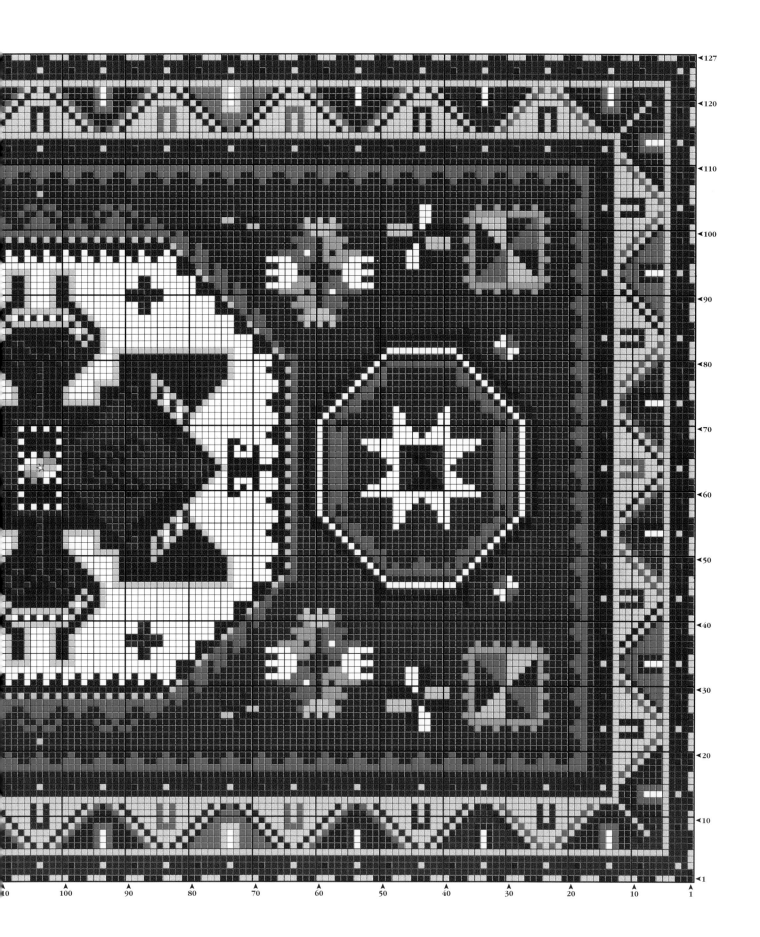

KAZAK RUG

CANVAS: 6# to the inch (2½# to the cm)

DESIGN AREA: 21 × 34 inches (53 × 86 cm)

STITCH: Cross

NEEDLE: Size 16

YARN: Appleton Tapestry, 2 threads (or Paternayan Persian, 3 strands, in square brackets on chart)

323	[512]	– 3 skeins	691	[444]	– 18 skeins
695	[732]	– 6 skeins	998	[221]	– 36 skeins
297	[660]	– 18 skeins	209	[D211]	– 54 skeins
882	[263]	– 18 skeins			

Quantities are for the rug worked in Appleton yarns.

If you would like to fringe the rug, you will need to buy cord, or you can use yarn (see page 122).

KAZAK BAG & STRAP

CANVAS: 8# to the inch (3# to the cm)

DESIGN AREA: 13 × 26 inches (33 × 66 cm)

The bag has two sides of 10½ × 13 inches (27 × 33 cm) with a flap of 5 inches (13 cm).

CANVAS REQUIRED: 17 × 30 inches (43 × 76 cm) plus 3 × 48 inches (8 × 122 cm) for the strap

STITCH: Cross

NEEDLE: Size 16

YARN: Appleton Tapestry, 1 thread (or Paternayan Persian, 2 strands, in square brackets on chart)

929	[510]	– 9 skeins	882	[263]	– 9 skeins
297	[660]	– 6 skeins	474	[725]	– 3 skeins
564	[584]	– 3 skeins	504	[950]	– 24 skeins

Quantities are for the bag shown, including the strap, worked in Appleton yarns.

For the strap, you can use whatever color yarns you have left after stitching the main part of the bag, or you can follow the chart.

STRAP: Starting with the central stripe, stitch a total of 7 stripes along the whole length. Leave ½ inch (1 cm) unworked at each end to stitch into the base of the bag. The center of the strap which goes over your shoulder looks best if it is stitched on both sides, so you need to increase the number of stripes in the middle of the strap by 3 on each side. Count up 74 stitches from each end (these sections form the gusset along each edge of the bag when it is finished) and then increase the width as described to 13 stripes. The 14th is the one which stitches the two edges of the central piece together (see below).

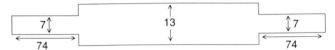

ASSEMBLY: The base of the bag is formed by the 5 rows of red background between the two smaller octagons and the blue edge of the octagons – 7 stitches in all.

Stitch the end of the strap to the outer edge of the bag exactly level with these 7 stitches. Use strong thread and backstitch, matching stitch for stitch. Then, matching the edges of the strap to the edges of the bag, continue stitching up the side of the bag for 74 stitches (the point at which the strap gets wider). To join the strap together in the middle, fold so that the raw edges overlap. Your final row of cross stitches must be made to go through two layers of canvas to create a perfect join.

A cotton lining can give your bag that little extra professional touch, including a pocket if desired. Make sure that at least one row of cross stitch is folded under at the front of the bag so that the lining is invisible on that edge when the bag is closed. You could also add a fastening such as the magnetic ones that you find on many handbags.

•

The bag was adapted from the Kazak rug.
The colors are slightly brighter and the canvas gauge is finer, making the size smaller. You can see how the strap forms the gusset. Shown here in a sporting atmosphere, the bag can be equally at home in more elegant surroundings.

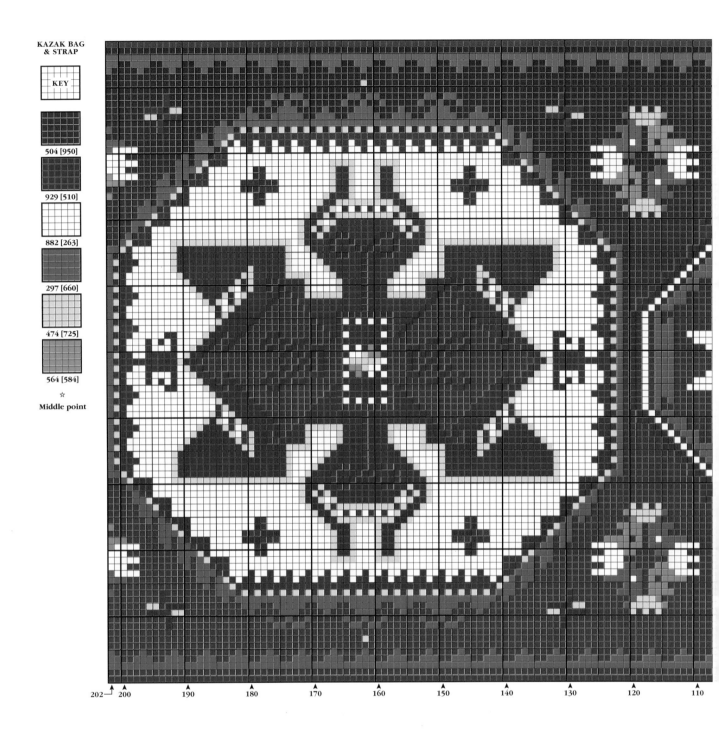

KAZAK BAG & STRAP

KEY

504 [950]

929 [510]

882 [263]

297 [660]

474 [725]

564 [584]

☆
Middle point

Repeat the design to this point to complete strap.

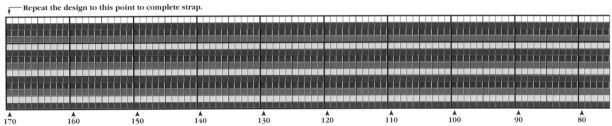

Center — These 7 rows form the base (attach handle here)

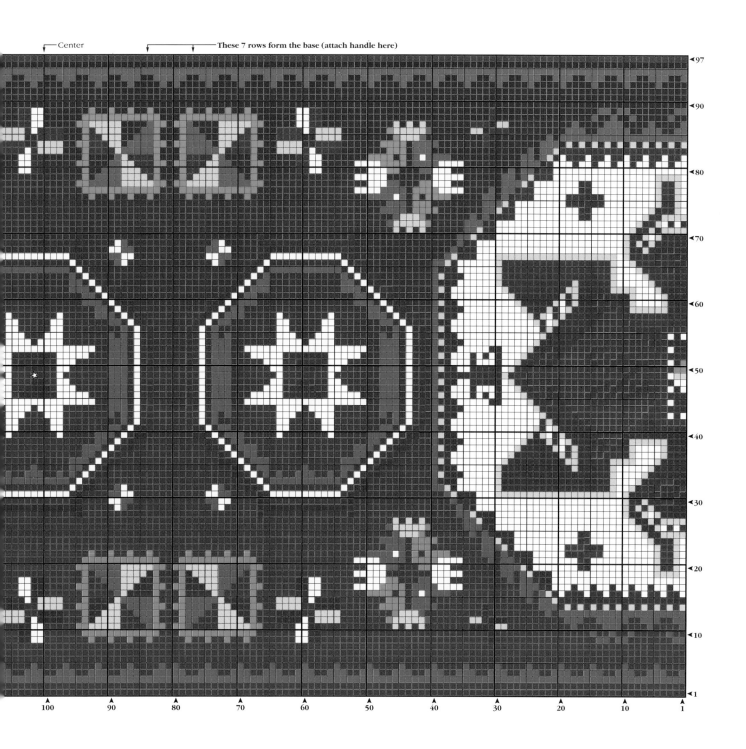

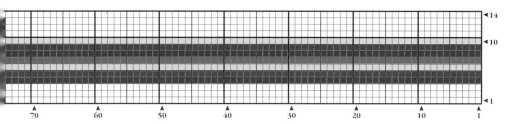

ANEMONES

ALTHOUGH MY TASTES usually run to more muted colors, anemones are one of my favorite flowers; I also like designs where the flowers or foliage overlap a border – in a similar way to the Jackfield Rose (page 48). When I saw a photograph of a beautiful Art Nouveau box lid from the early part of this century, I knew I had found the perfect combination. The wonderful array of colorful anemones had been painted by Lucia Mathews for the Furniture Shop, which she ran with her designer husband in San Francisco from 1906–1920.

I love the uninhibited air that anemones have, mixing mauves, fuchsias, and reds with such abandon. Every year I plant a few, and although each individual flower has a power and strength of its own, the naïveté of their vibrant colors is most evident when there are masses of blooms.

As you can see, there are several ways that you can use the chart – a pillow, a footstool, and a wonderfully delicate miniature (my favorite). A single flower could also be extracted and stitched on table napkins. A row of them, slightly overlapping, can be cross-stitched around a linen tablecloth. A rectangular stool top can be worked by stitching the design twice on canvas, side by side, and filling in the gaps at the top and bottom with some of the other flowers. Use the overlapping nature of the design to your advantage, and as long as you choose the individual flowers carefully, the result should look perfectly natural.

ANEMONES

CANVAS: 12# to the inch (5# to the cm)

DESIGN AREA: 10½ × 10½ inches (27 × 27 cm)

STITCH: Tent

NEEDLE: Size 18

YARN: Appleton Tapestry, 1 thread (or Paternayan Persian, 2 strands, in square brackets on chart)

447	[841]	– 3 skeins	991b	[260]	– 3 skeins
504	[950]	– 2 skeins	875	[236]	– 2 skeins
801	[353]	– 3 skeins	821	[543]	– 3 skeins
803	[351]	– 2 skeins	824	[540]	– 2 skeins
454	[301]	– 2 skeins	993	[220]	– 2 skeins
456	[300]	– 1 skein			
296	[600]	– 24 skeins (6 skeins for footstool)			

LINEN: 28# to the inch (11# to the cm)

DESIGN AREA: 4 × 4 inches (10 × 10 cm)

STITCH: Tent, with two strands over one intersection

NEEDLE: Size 24

THREAD: DMC Stranded Floss (in round brackets on the chart)

666	– 1 skein	Blanc	– 1 skein
498	– 1 skein	3072	– 1 skein
3608	– 1 skein	798	– 1 skein
3607	– 1 skein	796	– 1 skein
553	– 1 skein	310	– 1 skein
550	– 1 skein		

Mark out the background before stitching. The stool in the photograph is 10 inches (25 cm) in diameter. You will need to mark a circle using a string and pencil. Put the canvas on a board, tack some string to the center point of the canvas, tie a pencil to the other end the required distance away (half the proposed diameter), and draw a circle. Or you can place an appropriately sized plate on the canvas as close to the center as possible and trace a line around it. Find the center of the circle by folding the canvas in half horizontally, then vertically. The center is where the folds intersect.

•

The miniature version, looking so delicate,
is stitched on linen in stranded floss, showing the whole design.
(Overleaf) The pillow, footstool, and miniature are all shown together –
the vibrant colors light up the whole picture wonderfully. I do admire
these flowers, with their joie de vivre.

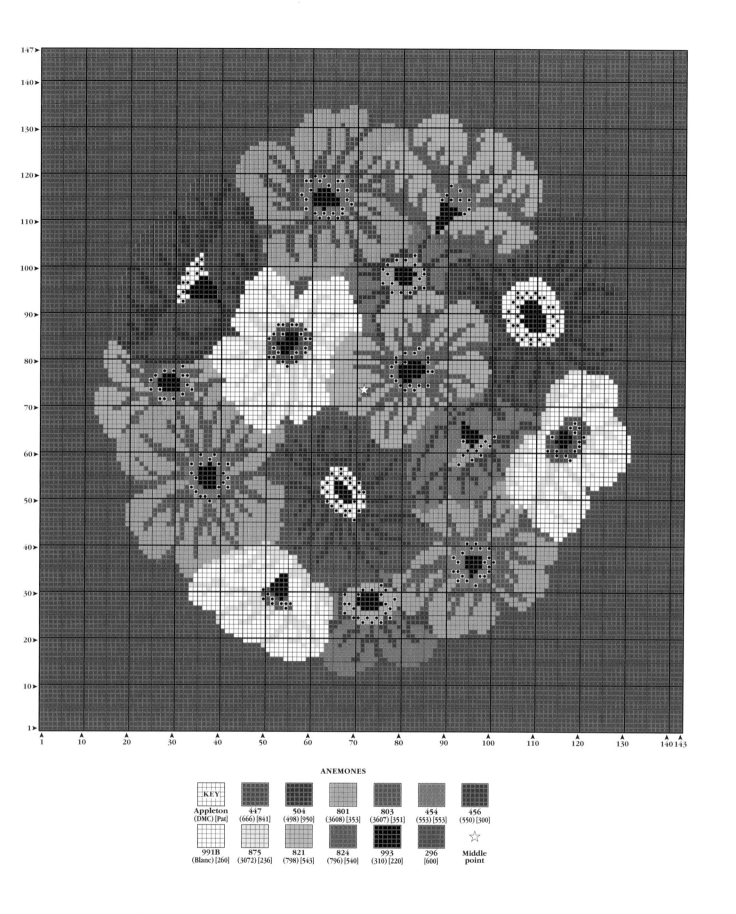

ANEMONES

KEY	447	504	801	803	454	456
Appleton (DMC) [Pat]	(666) [841]	(498) [950]	(3608) [353]	(3607) [351]	(553) [553]	(550) [300]

991B	875	821	824	993	296	Middle point
(Blanc) [260]	(3072) [236]	(798) [543]	(796) [540]	(310) [220]	[600]	☆

OWLS &
RABBITS

THESE MAKE ME smile every time I see them. The designs both belong to William De Morgan and were originally 6-inch tiles made close to Morris's Merton Abbey workshop. I've not been able to decide if the owls are drunk or just tired – or if the original was supposed to be a "stop-frame" of one owl in his demise. The colorings are mine, and in the cause of continuity, I added a branch or two.

The original Rabbits remind me of my childhood; of course, they shouldn't really be running around a branch. I'm afraid that De Morgan's originals, although definitely rabbits (I can tell by their ears), have rather odd bodies and lambs' tails, but with a little help from Julie Russell and Phyllis Steed, they are now young rabbits.

It seemed a shame not to use these designs in another way. Used as an individual owl or rabbit – on fine linen or canvas, a little owl or rabbit badge would be quite charming. Either could be worked on a pillowcase or blouse using waste canvas (see page 113). They could become a little "trademark" for a child; enough designs have been shown as miniatures in this book to allow you to imagine this.

The idea of a child's rug came to mind. The problem of how to position the Owls and Rabbits so that they lie in a logical way proved difficult; it was Angela Kahan who suggested mirror-imaging the Rabbits. This makes the rug suitable for the side of a child's bed, and the child can decide which way the rabbits should be facing, toward the bed or the room. This design also makes a lovely wallhanging, a throw for a toy box, or a double-width headboard. The rabbits are the same color, but the background was changed to look less sophisticated and more suitable for a child's room. You'll notice that the design overlaps the border unevenly (my husband's idea); this is to shorten the rug and improve the proportions. The border could also contain daisies or carrots or whatever you feel is appropriate. Should you use a border around the pillows, it will need to be even all around to make each a square.

Originally, the backgrounds for the pillows were worked (using gobelin filling stitch) in two shades of blue to depict the darkening sky, but as often happens, colors that looked

Tucked into the overmantel of a large, but dramatically simple, stone fireplace in Stanmore Hall the Owls are shown in the room with the Morris mosaic floor (see pages 66/67). We considered photographing the Owls at night on one of the turrets of the lovely Hall, but decided it was less practical.

different in the hand looked almost the same when stitched. My fault was in not working enough on my "rough" to see how it looked in reality. If you like the idea of this effect, I suggest that you spend a little time experimenting.

The humor of both the Owls and the Rabbits has given me enormous pleasure, both in the making and in the finished results.

OWLS PILLOW

CANVAS: 12# to the inch (5# to the cm)

DESIGN AREA: 13 × 13 inches (33 × 33 cm)

STITCH: (Design) Tent
(Background) Gobelin Filling or Tent

NEEDLE: Size 18

YARN: Appleton Tapestry, 1 thread (or Paternayan Persian, 2 strands, in square brackets on chart)

974 [462] – 2 skeins
911 [453] – 3 skeins
913 [433] – 3 skeins
304 [401] – 1 skein
761 [444] – 3 skeins
764 [413] – 2 skeins
882 [263] – 3 skeins
991 [261] – 1 skein
993 [220] – 1 skein
842 [734] – 1 skein
242 [652] – 2 skeins
335 [D511] – 2 skeins

Background: 926 [511] – 18 skeins

These are quantities for the pillow cover worked in Appleton yarns.

The background may be worked in tent stitch using one thread of tapestry yarn, or gobelin filling (as shown) using four threads of Appleton crewel yarn or 3 strands of Paternayan Persian. For stitch details, see page 118.

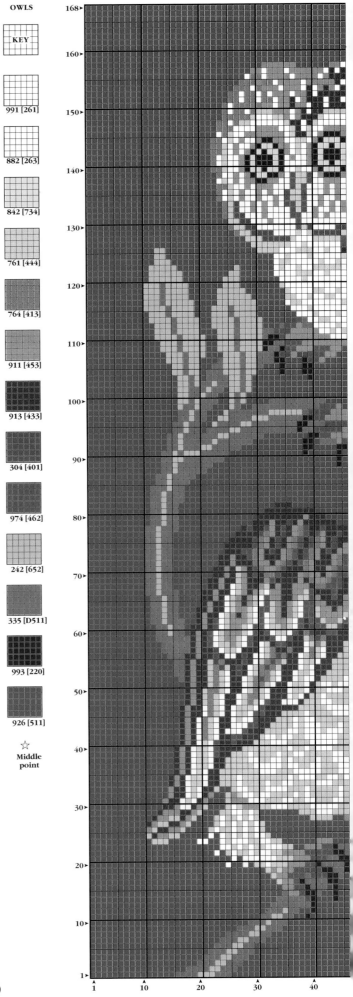

OWLS

KEY

991 [261]

882 [263]

842 [734]

761 [444]

764 [413]

911 [453]

913 [433]

304 [401]

974 [462]

242 [652]

335 [D511]

993 [220]

926 [511]

☆
Middle point

RABBITS PILLOW

CANVAS: 12# to the inch (5# to the cm)

DESIGN AREA: 13 × 13 inches (33 × 33 cm)

STITCH: (Design) Tent
(Background) Gobelin Filling or Tent

NEEDLE: Size 18

YARN: Appleton Tapestry, 1 thread (or Paternayan Persian, 2 strands, in square brackets on chart)

993	[220]	– 1 skein	762	[443]	– 2 skeins
972	[462]	– 1 skein	764	[413]	– 1 skein
913	[433]	– 1 skein	882	[263]	– 1 skein
984	[454]	– 2 skeins	241	[D531]	– 4 skeins
989	[246]	– 1 skein	242	[652]	– 3 skeins
761	[444]	– 2 skeins	335	[D511]	– 1 skein

Background: 926 [511] – 18 skeins

Quantities are for the pillow cover using Appleton yarns. Note that the greens are different from those in the rug: 353 on chart = 241, 355 = 242, 356 = 335.

The center point shown on the chart is for working the pillow.

The background can be worked in tent stitch using one thread of Appleton tapestry yarn or 2 strands of Paternayan Persian, or gobelin filling (as shown) using four threads of Appleton crewel yarn or 3 strands of Paternayan Persian. There is no border to the pillow; the background color extends two rows beyond the design.

•

The Rabbits, stitched on much coarser canvas and with the design "mirror-imaged" to form a charming rug. The background has been altered to suit a child's room.

RABBITS RUG

CANVAS: 6# to the inch (2½# to the cm)

DESIGN AREA: 28½ × 54 inches (72 × 137 cm)

STITCH: Cross

NEEDLE: Size 16

YARN: Appleton Tapestry, 2 threads (or Paternayan Persian, 3 strands, in square brackets on chart)

993	[220]	– 3 skeins
972	[462]	– 9 skeins
913	[433]	– 3 skeins
984	[454]	– 12 skeins
989	[246]	– 6 skeins
761	[444]	– 24 skeins
762	[443]	– 21 skeins
764	[413]	– 6 skeins
882	[263]	– 3 skeins
353	[604]	– 42 skeins
355	[603]	– 24 skeins
356	[601]	– 6 skeins

Background:
563	(555)	– 84 skeins
565	(583)	– 72 skeins

These are quantities for the rug worked in Appleton yarns.

The center point shown on the chart is for the pillow. The center of the rug is on the same line across, and on the far right-hand edge of the chart. The border shown on the chart is for the rug.

Note that the leaf greens and the background blues are different from those used in the pillow.

Mirror-imaging a design is easier for some people than for others. If you want to make the rug and find the problem too great, try taking a tracing of the first half when it has been worked and then retrace it in reverse on the other half of the canvas. The two halves probably will not match stitch for stitch, but the fact that the outlines are correct will help with the colors.

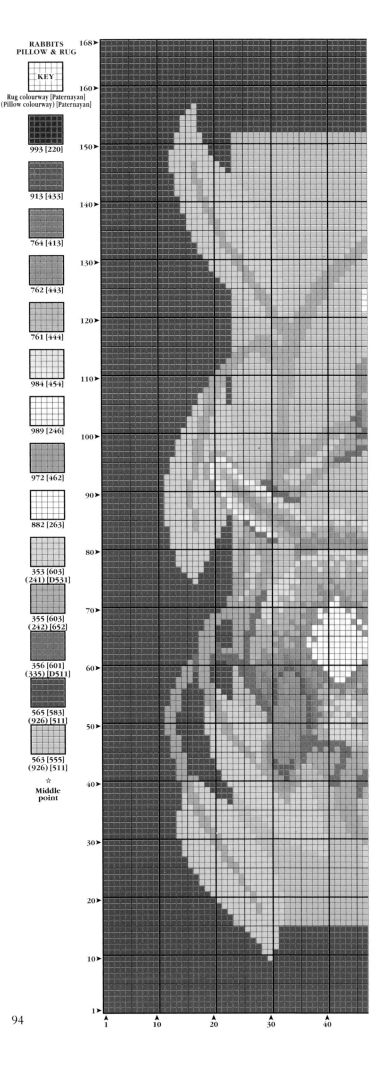

Light blue rectangle on rug only

Light blue rectangle on rug only

50 60 70 80 90 100 110 120 130 140 150 160 168

FROG & STORK

THIS IS ANOTHER of William De Morgan's amusing designs, although, as with quite a lot of his work, there is just a hint of menace. I feel sure that there must be a proverb or a cautionary tale to go with it. The slight apprehension of the Frog and the deceptive sleepiness of the Stork seem to need an explanation – we want to know what has happened before and what is going to happen next. Perhaps there is a chance here for Granny to weave some magic for her grandchildren while she stitches.

The original tile was produced with many different backgrounds, but the bulrushes help to put it into a setting. Many of De Morgan's tiles were monochromatic, and the coloring here is respectfully mine. The background gives a nice watery effect.

The stork actually looks like a cross between a Malibu stork and a heron; a real Malibu has an ugly red pouch under its beak, and a heron, which does feed on frogs, has backswept head feathers. All in all, it was better to stay as much as possible with the feel of the original as that was what De Morgan drew. Anyway, I rather like the hairstyle!

I considered adding this design to the Owls and Rabbits (page 88) to make a children's rug, but it was not similar enough in construction: it is upright, while the other two are rounder and might seem awkward with it.

The Frog is a strong enough character to make a pillow on his own. On 8#/inch (3#/cm) canvas, he becomes 8½ inches (21.5 cm) tall. He is stitched in cross stitch using one strand of tapestry yarn. Selina Winter felt that he looked a bit isolated floating in air, so she stitched him sitting on a stone. He could be in the puddle shown on the chart, or even on a leaf; it's up to you.

This would be a good beginner's project for children. The coarse canvas means it can be completed quickly, and the colors are complicated enough to be interesting, yet simple enough not to be too daunting. The subject matter should make it fun.

•

The two pillows appropriately shown near water. The Frog on his own has been stitched on coarser canvas, thereby increasing his size. It looks as if this larger Frog is casting a protective eye on his younger brother, who seems slightly under threat from the Stork.

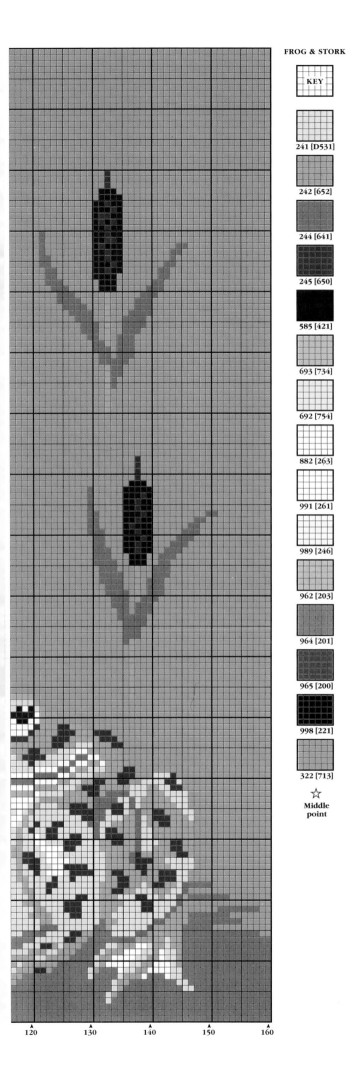

KEY

241 [D531]

242 [652]

244 [641]

245 [650]

585 [421]

693 [734]

692 [754]

882 [263]

991 [261]

989 [246]

962 [203]

964 [201]

965 [200]

998 [221]

322 [713]

☆
Middle point

120   130   140   150   160

FROG & STORK

FROG & STORK PILLOW

CANVAS: 12# to the inch (5# to the cm)

DESIGN AREA: 14 × 14 inches (35.5 × 35.5 cm)

STITCH: Tent

NEEDLE: Size 18

YARN: Appleton Tapestry, 1 thread (or Paternayan Persian, 2 strands, in square brackets on chart)

241	[D531]	– 1 skein	962	[203]	– 2 skeins
242	[652]	– 1 skein	964	[201]	– 3 skeins
244	[641]	– 1 skein	965	[200]	– 2 skeins
245	[650]	– 1 skein	998	[221]	– 1 skein
882	[263]	– 1 skein	991	[261]	– 1 skein
585	[421]	– 1 skein	692	[754]	– 1 skein
989	[246]	– 1 skein	693	[734]	– 1 skein

Background: 322 [513] – 16 skeins

FROG PILLOW

CANVAS: 8# to the inch (3# to the cm)

DESIGN AREA: 8½ × 9 inches (21.5 × 23 cm)

STITCH: Cross

NEEDLE: Size 16

YARN: Appleton Tapestry, 1 thread (or Paternayan Persian, 2 strands, in square brackets on chart)

241	[D531]	– 2 skeins	882	[263]	– 1 skein
242	[652]	– 2 skeins	998	[221]	– 1 skein
244	[641]	– 1 skein	991	[261]	– 1 skein
245	[650]	– 1 skein			

Background Crewel: 568 [500] – 21 skeins to make an area 13 inches (33 cm) square.

These are quantities for the two pillow covers worked in Appleton yarns.

The Frog on a stone is worked from one skein of Appleton Tapestry Wool 972 and three skeins of 974; use whatever colors and shapes take your fancy. My background is worked with four threads of Appleton Crewel Wool (or use 3 strands of Paternayan Persian) as this gives better coverage over a plain area.

If you want to add to the design or would just like to show more background, you will need more yarn (see page 113).

ANNIE JACKS

ANNIE JACKS, the wife of William Morris's chief furniture designer, was one of his main embroiderers. I have named these designs after her as it is believed that they were found in her house after her death; each is for a repeating fabric. I particularly wanted to see the many flowers in the large one in color.

In 1990 I was fortunate enough to have an exhibition of my work in Japan as part of a large promotion of British design. It provided the perfect excuse for deciding on the threads and having the designs stitched. The delicacy of cross stitch on linen seemed more suitable than needlepoint, although the design restrictions are the same for both.

The threads we used are Danish Flower Threads. I was not totally familiar with the color choice and unfortunately did not have enough time to try out variations before the exhibition. I would like to play with the yellows and greens in the large piece; you, with the design charted, are free to explore all the possibilities.

It would be interesting to use elements of this design separately: the daisies as a group or a stem of fritillaries. It was most enjoyable seeing this design come to life.

The other two antique drawings, which repeat a single flower, both have a corner which had been painted. These two corners have been extracted from the overall design and stitched with Danish Flower Threads that match the original colors – the coral flower on linen and the yellow flower on dark-colored Aida imitate the painted background. Their simplicity is lovely and would work just as well on much coarser canvas.

ANNIE JACKS

LARGER PIECE:
EVENWEAVE LINEN: 28# to the inch (11# to the cm)
or AIDA: 14# to the inch (5½# to the cm)

STITCH: Cross, with 1 thread

NEEDLE: Size 22 or 24

YARN: Danish Flower Threads

DESIGN AREA: 14 × 24 inches (36 × 61 cm)

Fritillaries –		Aconites –		Daisy Petals –	
	3		6		0
	4		46		19
	11		203	Leaves –	101
	14		225		212
	29	Bluebells –	21		238
	235		22		302
			227		
			228		

The three designs found at the house of Annie Jacks. These three are all repeating designs and would be suitable for printed fabrics.

The patches of color from the two simpler designs have been reproduced as small cross-stitch pictures. The more complex design has been completely embroidered.

ANNIE JACKS

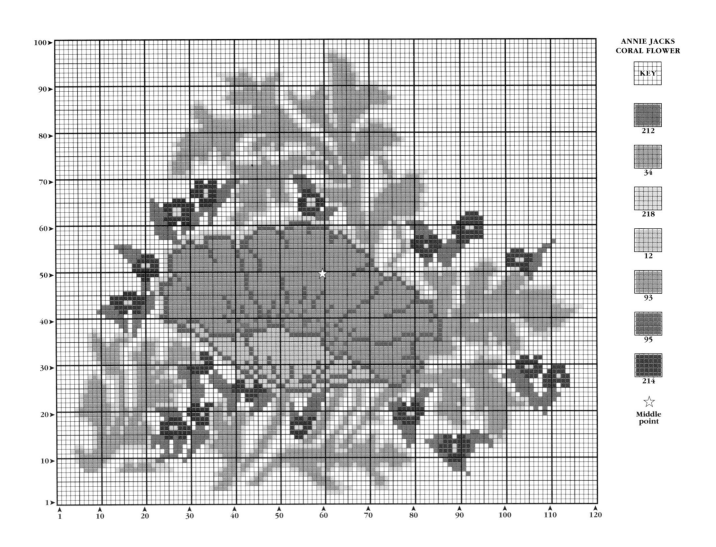

SMALLER PIECES:

CORAL FLOWER (LINEN)

DESIGN AREA: 6½ × 7½ inches (16.5 × 19 cm)

YARN: Danish Flower Threads

12	212
34	214
93	218
95	

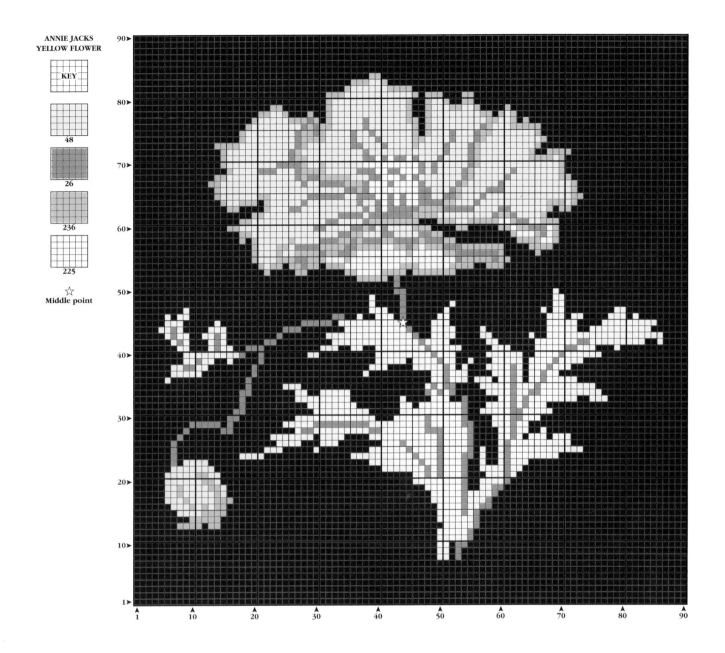

**ANNIE JACKS
YELLOW FLOWER**

KEY

48

26

236

225

☆
Middle point

YELLOW FLOWER (BLUE AIDA)

DESIGN AREA: 5½ × 6½ inches (14 × 16 cm)

YARN: Danish Flower Threads

26	225
48	236

These designs are worked in cross stitch, using one thread
over two intersections of the linen, or one thread over one
intersection of the Aida.

107

BIRD & LEAF

THIS PRETTY DESIGN, inspired by a silk and wool fabric created by C. F. A. Voysey in 1899, lends itself to more applications than most. Originally I had thought of it as a bolster, with just one more line of leaves. To do this, you might omit the last blue bird on the right, replace it with the diving brown one on the far left, and then continue stitching that group.

The birds are varied in their sizes, but are quite amusing and interchangeable. I have never seen the original Voysey version in color, and because his birds are very stylized, I have had to invent. House martins were chosen, with sand martins added to vary the colors. Each type flies in a group, with another bird or two slightly out of formation and swooping to rejoin friends. It was fascinating to play with the positioning of the birds and decide on the arrangement of the colors.

All the design elements in Voysey's original are outlined and feature an irregular striped background which gives the impression of waves of water or a hazy sky. I tried to retain this feel, but, as a background worked in long stitch has a tendency to obscure the edges of the design, I used the outlining to help the birds stand out, working them in tent stitch with the darker of the background blues. Upon reflection, I think that the leaves could have benefitted from the same treatment.

The problem with the color of the background was finding two blues which would give an illusion of sky or water; they needed to be close in shade, but distinguishable from one another. The best solution was to use one solid color for one stripe and to blend it with a lighter shade for the other.

If you wish to make a bellpull, use the chart and replace the bottom leaf with the top one which gently twists into the center leaf. The birds could be as they are in the right-hand fall of leaves, or they could be varied. With the chart you have freedom to experiment.

The design might also be used to make a very pretty curtain pelmet, either by using the three central leaves as they are and adjusting the birds – or by twisting the design, again using one fall of leaves, this time horizontally, and adjusting the birds. You will need to count carefully to make sure that the birds you have chosen will fit or perhaps overlap the leaves. They will, of course, need to be flying horizontally!

•

Stylized birds are a recurring theme in Voysey's work; mine are more realistic and colorful. They look as if they are flying to freedom.

BIRD & LEAF PILLOW

CANVAS: 14# to the inch (5½# to the cm)

DESIGN AREA: 13 × 13 inches (33 × 33 cm)

STITCH: Tent

NEEDLE: Size 20

YARN: Appleton Crewel, 3 threads (or Paternayan Persian, in square brackets on chart, 2 strands)

873	[615]	– 2 skeins
874	[624]	– 2 skeins
352	[605]	– 5 skeins
401	[613]	– 5 skeins
293	[603]	– 2 skeins
294	[601]	– 2 skeins
762	[443]	– 2 skeins
991b	[260]	– 1 skein
974	[462]	– 1 skein
852	[570]	– 1 skein
929	[510]	– 2 skeins
926	[511]	– 2 skeins
993	[220]	– 1 skein
882	[263]	– 1 skein
588	[420]	– 1 skein
986	[453]	– 1 skein
185	[431]	– 2 skeins
187	[430]	– 1 skein

Background:

876	[213]	– 4 skeins
561	[505]	– 11 skeins

These are quantities for the pillow cover worked in Appleton yarns.

One row of tent stitch in Appleton 561 is worked around the birds to give them a clearly defined outline.

Stitch the whites of the eyes last, using white sewing thread on top of the black stitches.

I worked the background in Appleton crewel yarns in alternate rows, blending 1 thread of 561 and 2 of 876 in the needle for one row and using 3 threads of 561 on its own for the next (see page 120). Or use 1 strand each of Paternayan 213 and 505 for the first row, and work the next using 2 strands of 505.

Three rows of tent stitch in Appleton 561 are worked around the whole design.

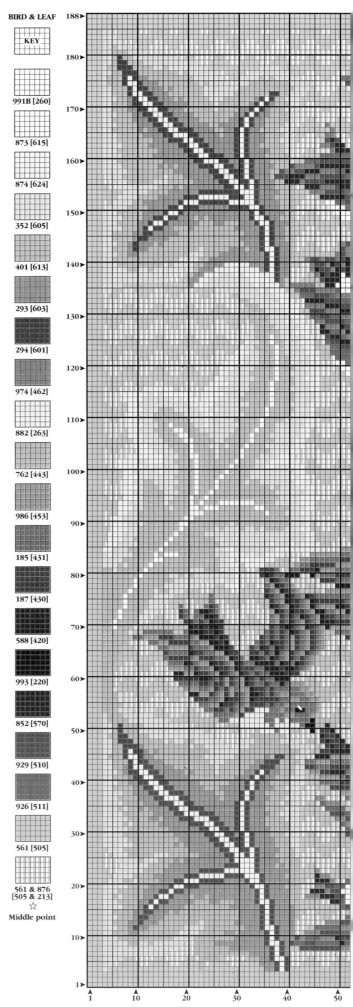

BIRD & LEAF

KEY

991B [260]
873 [615]
874 [624]
352 [605]
401 [613]
293 [603]
294 [601]
974 [462]
882 [263]
762 [443]
986 [453]
185 [431]
187 [430]
588 [420]
993 [220]
852 [570]
929 [510]
926 [511]
561 [505]
561 & 876
[505 & 213]
☆
Middle point

BASIC
TECHNIQUES

HOPEFULLY YOU NOW feel enthusiastic about starting a new project. My aim is that, even if you decide to start on the simplest piece and not alter anything from my original, you will soon be confident enough to adapt and change as much as I know I would.

Choose carefully. Preferably it will be something you need, something that will enhance your decor, or maybe a gift (but only for someone who will appreciate it). It has to be something that you will really want to complete.

This decision will need to be followed by others: the size and then the colors. With this fairly broad picture, you move on to the fun of buying the materials. At this stage you might prefer to buy small quantities and try them out. If you are intending to change anything drastically, especially the colors, I would strongly recommend that you do some experimenting.

The basic steps, after you have decided on your design and its purpose, are as follows:

(a) assessing the correct gauge and size of canvas or other fabric (see page 116 for calculating sizes from charts)
(b) choosing the most suitable threads, both type and color
(c) finding the correct needle
(d) understanding charts
(e) marking the background
(f) deciding whether to use a frame and which kind
(g) stitching and how to start and tie off
(h) finishing your stitched work
(i) the moment of truth – its final display.

All of these points are discussed in the pages that follow. I hope that they do not sound too much like a teaching manual, but it is important to be disciplined in your choices at the outset. For instance, nothing is more demoralizing than putting in several hours of stitching, only to discover that the piece of canvas you have been using is too small. That happened to me – but only once.

Remember that your project is unique: only you have stitched it. A small deviation from the way that I have done things is not necessarily a mistake; instead, it is your own personal contribution to the finished piece. There is no "totally wrong" nor "totally right" way in these matters, only enjoyment. If you are not enjoying what you are doing, you need to rethink the design. Perhaps you can find a simpler way to complete the piece, or choose more inspiring colors.

MATERIALS

CANVAS AND FABRIC

CANVAS Most of the pieces in this book have been stitched on canvas, either mono or rug interlock. For my kits, I prefer to use high-quality polished deluxe mono canvas, both because its smoothness does not roughen the threads and because of its strength. If a canvas is badly out of shape after stitching, as sometimes happens, the stretching of the dampened finished canvas will need to be quite drastic; weak canvas can tear. Rug canvas is inherently quite heavy and strong; the stretching here should be minimal, as I advocate cross stitch for all my rugs to limit distortion.

Canvas comes in different widths and thread counts (#). The more threads there are to the inch (cm), the more stitches to the inch (cm). Thus, a finer canvas will take longer to stitch, but will enable you to show more detail. The finer the canvas is, of course, the finer the thread needed to stitch it.

Always buy the best-quality canvas that you can afford – your time is the most valuable part of any work – and make sure that it is large enough to accommodate your design.

SIZE Decide at the outset what size you want your finished piece to be. Whether it is the same as the samples that I have shown, or whether you want to extend the background (see Threads below) to make a larger pillow or a special shape such as a chair seat, you will need at least 2 inches (5cm) all around your stitched area to allow for "stretching" or "blocking" when you have finished.

Remember, if you choose a gauge of canvas that is coarser than that used for the samples, the design will finish up larger and you will need an appropriate piece of canvas to accommodate it. See page 116 for how to calculate.

LINEN Linen has been used with several of the designs to show how different a design can look on another medium.

The type of linen produced for counted embroidery is called "evenweave." It has the same number of warp and weft threads to the inch (or cm). The weave is like mono canvas, although the threads are never absolutely smooth and usually have a natural slub. It is available in different gauges, all rather fine, of which 28# to the inch (11# to the cm) is probably the most commonly used.

As the background is rarely stitched and as linen is slightly transparent, threads at the back can be seen from the front of the work. It is therefore important that the thread be finished off after each block of stitching. The fabric is much softer than canvas, so it is easier to work on a frame or in a hoop.

AIDA This is a cotton fabric, the threads of which are woven very evenly; this makes it ideally suited for counted work. Cross stitch is made over one intersection. Aida is not as see-through as linen or canvas because the fabric is somewhat denser. It is still not advisable, especially with lighter colored Aida, to run threads across the back between the stitching. Again, a hoop is a good idea to keep the fabric taut.

WASTE CANVAS This is a loose evenweave fabric with fine threads. Its purpose is to enable you to transfer a counted design onto an otherwise unsuitable fabric. A piece of the canvas is basted lightly onto the main fabric where the design is to be placed. The stitches are counted from a chart in the normal way, but the needle must pass through the canvas hole (not snagging the canvas) and through the fabric underneath. Pull the thread slightly tighter than usual. When the stitching is complete, the canvas threads and basting are gently withdrawn, leaving the design miraculously on your suede collar or silk shirt.

THREADS

All my thinking is done in Appleton colors. Years of familiarity have made it easy to identify which Appleton number will most closely resemble the shade I am looking for. Therefore, all the yarn used in these design samples are the same brand. If you prefer to use, or can more easily find, another brand of yarn, conversion charts are available from manufacturers, and embroidery retailers usually have shade cards. Also included are alternative colors for each project in Paternayan yarn, but bear in mind that the finished piece will look different and quantities of yarn needed may vary from the ones stated.

Both Appleton Crewel and Tapestry Wools come in the same choice of numbered colors.

CREWEL WOOL is 2-ply fine yarn suitable for any gauge of canvas and necessary for finer canvas, such as 18# or 14#, and for blending colors. Many believe that because several strands need to be used at the same time in the needle, this yarn lies flatter than Tapestry Wool.

TAPESTRY WOOL is a thicker 4-ply yarn, usually used as a single strand (unless you are working on a very coarse canvas). The thickness is equivalent to 3 strands of Crewel; its advantage is that you only need one thread in the needle. The disadvantage is that the subtle blending of shades is not possible, and if a different stitch is being used for the background, it might not cover the canvas.

Appleton wool is sold in hanks (about 1 ounce/25 grams) or smaller skeins. As a general guide, one hank will cover 36 square inches (232 square cms) or 6 × 6 inches (15 × 15 cm) working in tent stitch on 18#, 14#, or 12# to the inch canvas (7#, 5½#, or 5# to the cm).

Paternayan Persian is a stranded wool yarn that can be divided into three separate threads. A single strand can be used instead of two strands of Appleton Crewel; two strands can be substituted for one thread of Appleton Tapestry. In this book, Paternayan numbers are shown in brackets after the equivalent Appleton number.

If you wish to increase the size of your project by working on a larger gauge of canvas, increasing the background area, or adding a border, you will need more yarn than specified. Ideally it is best to learn your own needs by noting how much you cover with a particular stitch on your chosen canvas with a measured length of yarn. (If you have not done any stitching before, use the method above and try to note if the specified amount is correct for you.)

To allow for any dye changes, it is advisable to get all your background yarn at the same time. If you cannot do this, make sure that you do not run out completely. Then some of the original purchase can be blended with the new in the needle for a few rows, making the change so gradual as to be unnoticeable. This is, of course, not possible if you are using only one thread of Tapestry Wool in your needle. Try it out for yourself. The instructions for each design state what was actually used, but this may not suit you.

After you have bought your canvas and before deciding on the threads, it is always best to try a few stitches to see how your tension covers the canvas. This will help you decide which yarn you want, and if you are working out your own color scheme, you will certainly need to stitch the shades together to see if they work as you expected. Stitched threads have a quite different effect on each other from ones that you just hold in the hand. The Owls and Rabbits with their two shades of background prove that!

COTTON THREADS Out of the very many different sorts and makes available, I have contented myself with just two – both sold in skeins. Stranded floss comes in a large choice of colors from several manufacturers. They are all six-stranded threads and have a sheen rather like silk. Danish Flower Threads have a limited, but surprisingly versatile choice of soft colors reminiscent of the vegetable dyes once used to make them. They are single-stranded and soft-textured with no sheen.

NUMBER OF THREADS

Again, with each set of instructions, I have specified the number of threads used in the needle to cover the canvas or to achieve the blending that was required. However, different stitchers work with different tensions; some pull more tightly than others, and this can affect the thickness of the thread needed. There are a few golden rules that might make things easier.

The thread(s) should pull easily through the canvas with no tugging, and when a block of stitches has been completed, no canvas should be "grinning" through. If you can achieve this and a nice even tension, you are on your way to excellence. The tension is the key. A tight tension will, of course, pull the yarn and cause it to be thinner; a too-tight tension might distort the canvas unless it is well framed. Professionals who work very fast on very taut frames tend to have a tight tension; they will always need the maximum thickness of thread to cover the canvas. A newcomer working in the hand needs to avoid pulling too tightly, so many find a thinner thread adequate to cover their canvas. It is up to each stitcher to decide as an individual.

The cover for the gauge of canvas used for my designs that is most open to discussion is 14#/inch (5½#/cm). Many people use three threads of Crewel Wool (or one of Tapestry); others find this too tight and are happier with two threads of Crewel. Working in cross stitch on 8#/inch (3#/cm), some are happier with one thread of Tapestry Wool, others with four threads of Crewel.

The thickness of the thread is also affected by the type of stitch. A straight stitch over, say, four intersections of canvas will need a thicker thread to cover the canvas than tent stitch on the same canvas. Therefore, if you have chosen Tapestry Wool for the design, you may need to use Crewel for the background, where an extra thread can easily be added for the long stitch. Do not worry about using some Tapestry Wool and some Crewel on the same piece – you will not notice the difference.

A table of canvas gauges, yarn, and stitches used in this book appears on page 123.

NEEDLES

Blunt-ended tapestry needles with long, easily threaded eyes are best. Size 16 is suitable for rug canvas and will take two threads of Tapestry Wool if needed. Size 18 is best for 12#/inch (5#/cm) canvas; size 20 for 14#/inch (5½#/cm), and size 22 for 18#/inch (7#/cm). The rule of thumb is that the needle should be easy to thread with the appropriate amount of yarn and easy to pull through the canvas.

To thread a needle, fold the threads around the needle and pinch tight. Slide them off the needle while pinching them, then push the fold of threads through the eye.

STITCHING

This can be done by using either one or both hands. If a frame is used, the needle can be passed through the canvas from one hand to the other, forming a stitch each time it travels up and down. This can be done incredibly quickly by experienced stitchers, and people used to this technique are generally reluctant to change. Sometimes one hand is used to insert the needle and the same hand is used to pull it out under the work and replace it. As the hand has to move from over to under the canvas continuously, this method is slower. A faster way to stitch with one hand is better done without a frame, as the canvas needs to be pliable. Each placing of the needle inserts it into one hole and, in the same movement, out of the next. (See page 118 [tent stitch]). The hand needs only to move to the pointed end of the needle to extract it; then repeat the movement. This is very useful for the middle of large pieces, where getting both hands and arms around yards of canvas can be exhausting. A word of warning about this last method: try not to pull too tightly. The canvas is already slightly bent by the action of the needle entering and leaving at the same time, and if you pull, you will distort the canvas. Just keep the action gentle and the tension even. After a while, you will slip into a rhythm, which will make it much easier.

The order of stitching is important. Be sure that the foreground details are correct before you begin working on the background. On printed canvases, it is crucial. The overlying parts of the design must be stitched first to give them clear outlines. I like to be able to work colors as I get to them and find it quicker and much less distracting if I have several needles threaded with different colors ready at the same time.

STARTING AND FINISHING

It is neater (and you'll find it easier) if the threads are finished off at the back by being held down by other stitches. An easy way to achieve this is to knot the thread and take it down from the right side of the canvas an inch or so away from where you will start. Position the knot so that you will be working toward it with the same or similar colored yarn. You will find that when you reach the knot, the thread will be woven in behind, and the knot can safely be cut off. You can finish off similarly by bringing the end of the thread up a little distance from your work and, when you have stitched up to it, it will be tightly woven in. To thread through the stitches at the back has the same effect, but it means turning the canvas over – not always easy on a frame.

Knots on the wrong side of your work have two

The front of this canvas looks impeccable!

disadvantages. One is that they sometimes get entangled with your stitching, which is a nuisance; also they might cause bumps on the right side when your work is finished and stretched.

CHARTS

For those who already favor following charts (rather than stitching onto a painted or printed canvas), I have nothing to add. To the uninitiated, I must warn you that stitching from charts can become an addiction!

All the charts in this book have been produced by Ethan Danielson, whose wizardry with the computer has given us both the beauty of art and the precision of science. Each color on the chart represents one color of thread, and each square represents one stitch.

It is always best to start working in good daylight. Sort the yarn into colors and identify which square in the index they represent. If the colors are very close – they are in Fox, for instance – note in the good daylight where they are positioned.

Find the center mark on the chart (normally it will correspond with the center of the canvas, but see the paragraph below). Find the canvas center by folding it in half in each direction – the intersection is the center. I prefer to mark these intersecting lines by basting along them with bright sewing thread, as it helps to dissect the chart and gives more points of reference from which to count.

Not everyone likes to start from the center. If you do not, it is essential to make sure that the design is going to fit within your chosen canvas area. It is possible that the center of the canvas is not where you will want to place the center of the design. In the case of a chair seat with a larger drop at the front than the back, for instance, you will want the design to appear in the center of the seat. Or, possibly, a repeat of the design will be called for on a long stool. Or, with Woodpecker, you may only want to use part of the design to fit a squarer shape. Whatever your chosen design, careful planning pays enormous dividends.

The boon of charts is their versatility. You can, of course, follow the exact formula given in the book and you will know how your finished work should look. But, more important, with a chart you can adapt the design to your precise needs. In this book I hope that I have given you a small taste of what can be achieved.

The design size may be reduced or increased by changing the gauge of the canvas, by increasing or eliminating the background, by adding borders, or by extending the design itself (as with the Fox and Hare chair seats). The colors can be changed, as can the materials used – and, naturally, you need only stitch the part you like best.

To calculate how a design will alter its size on a different canvas, take the number of stitches on the chart and divide that number by the gauge of the canvas; this will give you the eventual size. For example, 140 stitches will measure 14 inches on a 10#/inch canvas (35 cm on 4#/cm). On an 18#/inch canvas it will measure just under 8 inches (20 cm on 7#/cm).

$$\frac{\text{Number of Stitches}}{\text{Gauge of Canvas}} = \text{Size of Design} \quad \frac{140}{10} = 14$$

Do not forget the extra canvas you will need around the design.

On linen the same principle applies, but using cross stitch over two intersections effectively halves the gauge – a 28#/inch (11#/cm) linen counts as 14# (5½#). Therefore, the same design with 140 stitches will measure 10 inches (25 cm) if worked in cross stitch over two intersections of 28#/inch (11#/cm) linen, and 5 inches (12.5 cm) if tent stitch is used over one intersection.

The Hare chair seat (see pages 26/27), showing the extra stitching and shape required

SPECIAL SHAPES

After choosing the canvas, check carefully that you have enough threads in both directions to accommodate the number of stitches in your design (plus the 2 inches [5 cm] all around for stretching). If you are making an unusually shaped piece, you will also need to mark the background area before you start. This is not necessary if you have just decided to work a few rows around the design in straight lines, but if the area is curved, or if you need to leave some parts unstitched so that the piece will sit well around the leg of a stool, it is almost impossible to do this accurately at a later stage – either because the canvas is on a frame or because it has already gone a little out of shape.

TEMPLATES A good upholsterer can make a template for you; this is simply a piece of paper or cloth (muslin is perfect) cut to the exact shape you need to cover with your stitching, so it is not too difficult to do yourself. The outline should be drawn onto the canvas before you do anything else. If a piece of furniture is being recovered, it is possible to use the old cover as a template. Any re-upholstering or re-stuffing should be done before you establish the final shape so, if you use the old fabric, check that it is still the right size. Lay the fabric over the area to be covered, smooth the cloth flat, hold in place with pins, and mark with a pencil where your stitching will need to end. Mark around legs which protrude into the design area. Make a mark where you want the center of your design to fall.

Remove the template, check that the lines are symmetrical (often simply by folding it in half) and if not, check the upholstery again before cutting along the line you have drawn. Lay the template on the canvas; the canvas threads should follow the vertical and horizontal lines of the template to make sure that the design will not be lopsided.

Make sure, too, that the center mark of the template is also marked on the canvas, as this is where you will want the center of the design to lie. If you are going to stitch two designs on a long stool, for instance, you might want to count the threads before deciding exactly where the centers of the designs should be.

Mark the canvas around the edges of the template with either a running stitch in colored sewing thread or an indelible pen. Your background needs to be stitched to this line. However, the canvas should extend, even at the closest points, 2 inches (5 cm) or more all around. The canvas must not be cut until the stitching and stretching are done and then, ideally, by your upholsterer.

FRAMES

Some of the advantages of working on a frame will have become apparent from the stitching section above. Frames hold the work flat and under tension so that both hands can be used to stitch. They also help the work retain a better shape, making the stretching procedure, when the work is finished, easier.

There are many ways of framing, from the traditional scroll or slate frame which allows the canvas to be held very tightly, to attaching the canvas to an old picture frame with thumbtacks. In theory, the width of the frame should be wider than the total width of the unworked canvas. In a scroll frame, where the canvas is sewn to tapes attached to the top and bottom bars, the canvas should not be wider than the length of the tape. If the width is correct (the canvas can be narrower), the length does not matter, as it can be rolled around one of the bars at the top or bottom.

For very large pieces, such as a rug, where you might find a full-sized frame impractical, the canvas can be pinned to a smaller frame so that the part being worked is within the frame area. When a section is completed, the canvas can be moved and re-pinned. This can be done with a scroll frame, an old picture frame, or a stretcher frame. You will not get the canvas very tight, but it means you will be able to use both hands; loose canvas should be rolled to allow you to reach under the frame.

A hoop or round frame can be used for small or large projects. Again, the hoop is moved from one part of the canvas or fabric to another. It can be difficult to fit partially worked canvas pieces onto a hoop as they can be stiff. However, with a little perseverance, it can be done, though the hoop should be removed when you have finished stitching for the day. The larger the ring, the easier it is to accommodate coarser gauges of canvas.

Hoops consist of two rings, one of them expandable by means of a screw or spring. The fabric is laid across the smaller ring and, with the screw loosened sufficiently, the larger one is pressed over the fabric and around the under ring; the screw is then tightened. The fabric may need to be pulled gently from the edges to make it taut before the screw is made very tight. You can obtain hoops just as rings or with a mechanism to attach them to a table or floor stand.

Square frames can be found in varying weights from the strong scroll frame to much lighter travel frames. They work on the same principle, but you will not be able to achieve the same degree of tightness on a travel frame.

There are now many forms of stands for both square and round frames. Some are very elegant pieces of furniture; others resemble something invented by a mad scientist, with joints and bolts everywhere to make the stand more adjustable to each person's needs.

Before you choose, it is obviously ideal if you can try one, or at least sit with it so that you can feel the weight; imagine where you will keep it at home. Many good embroidery stores will have one or two frames set up.

FIXING YOUR CANVAS TO A FRAME

How a hoop works is described above. Hoops are ideal for linen or Aida. They are extremely easy to use and light in weight.

A travel or lightweight square frame needs to have the canvas attached to the webbing at top and bottom; the webbing must be wider than the canvas. Find the center of the webbing, match it with the center of the canvas, and hem-stitch in place. The side bars are never very long, and you will almost always have to roll the canvas around the bars at top or bottom, depending on which part of the canvas you are working on. The rollers are held to the bars by wing nuts; these tend to slip, so it is not possible to hold the canvas very tight.

With a scroll frame, you can stretch the canvas very tightly as it can be pulled in both directions. Sew a strip of webbing along the two sides of canvas. Do not hem the canvas; this will cause a thickness along the edge which will prevent the canvas from pulling tight when it is rolled. The webbing can be stitched by machine if you wish. Match the center of the top and bottom of the canvas to the centers of the webbing attached to the frame rollers. Fold the canvas back, then stitch from the center to the sides very firmly with button thread. It is absolutely essential that the frame holds

Table-standing hoop

Square scroll frame

the canvas perfectly square.

When you have inserted the side slats into the rollers, see that the pegs are in the same position on each side – the holes are evenly spaced. You may need to roll the canvas around either the top or bottom roller bar (Woodpecker, for instance, would certainly need to be rolled). Similarly, see that the pegs are in the same holes on each side. Attach string very securely by tying to the top of the side slat and roller, and using a large-eyed needle, loop the string at regular intervals around the side slat and through the webbing. Pull very tightly and attach securely. This stringing may have to be removed and replaced as you reposition the canvas to complete the stitching. It can be drum-tight; once you have stitched well-framed canvas using both hands, you will understand why people are prepared to go to all this trouble.

TYPES OF STITCHES

For each of the main worked samples throughout this book, I have specified which type of stitch was used. The most common of these are tent stitch, for those worked on finer canvas such as the pillows and chair seats, and cross stitch where coarser canvas is used for such items as rugs. Cross stitch is also used for the alternative examples worked on linen (see below.)

Interesting effects can often be achieved by using more decorative long stitches for the background areas. Gobelin filling stitch is one that I have used; for others, check one of the many good books devoted entirely to the many types of needlepoint stitches.

TENT STITCH

This is a diagonal stitch, which forms a long stitch on the back of the canvas. It has the advantage of being a small stitch; as it goes over only one thread of the canvas, design details can be depicted easily, and it will wear well. It has the disadvantage, since it pulls only in one direction, of distorting the shape of the canvas. This means that you will need to stretch your work before making it up into a finished piece.

The stitching may be horizontal across the canvas backwards and forwards or down and up if you wish. If you are not using a frame, you can turn the canvas at the end of a row so that you always work from right to left or top to bottom (reverse if you are left-handed). If you are using a frame and both hands, there is no need to turn the canvas; just return along the next row, still putting the needle up through the stitch hole above and putting it down through the hole below and diagonally to the left. Continue along the row from left to right.

Tent stitch may also be worked in diagonal lines; this method is also called basketweave. This distorts the canvas

much less and gives a very firm back to your work; I recommend it for backgrounds as it also gives a smooth finish. It is essential that you work alternately from top to bottom and then the reverse. Two rows in the same direction cause a break in the weave at the back which will show on the front. To help you remember the direction in which the last row was worked, always leave a thread hanging from your last stitch.

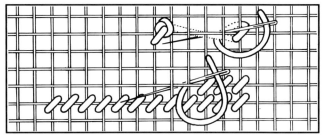

TENT STITCH worked horizontally (turn canvas for 2nd row)

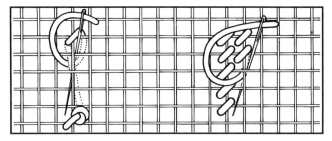

TENT STITCH worked vertically (turn canvas for 2nd row)

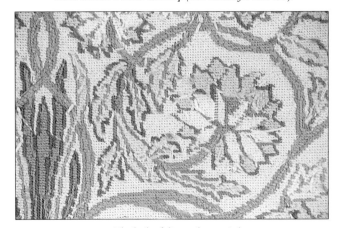

The back of diagonal tent stitch

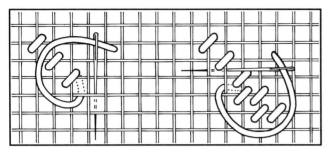

BASKETWEAVE

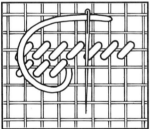

The back of basketweave

CROSS STITCH

This has been used for all the rugs in the book. It has the advantages of being hard-wearing as well as helping the canvas hold its shape, since there are pulls in opposite directions with each stitch.

There are many ways of executing the stitch. All are correct, but you must find the one that suits you best. The most common way is to work the required number of stitches in half-cross, then return along them completing the crosses. Most people also use half-cross stitch for the second part of the cross, so that only a short stitch can be seen at the back of the work. However, others are happier with tent stitch as the second row. This gives both a long stitch and a good padding on the back, but may pull the canvas unevenly, causing it to need stretching. Other people prefer to complete each individual cross before starting the next, either by using the methods described above, or by placing the needle both in and out of the canvas in one horizontal movement.

No matter which method you use, it is imperative that all the top stitches lie in the same direction to give a smooth and professional look.

Half-cross stitch gives the same appearance on the front, but has a short stitch on the back. It is really suitable only for interlock canvas because interlock will not allow the stitches to slip between the weave, which can happen with normal mono canvas.

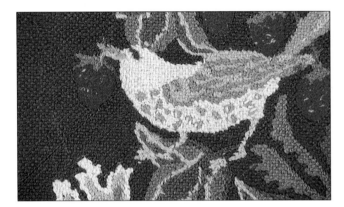

HALF CROSS STITCH   *CROSS STITCH*

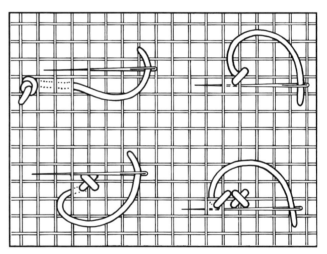

CROSS STITCH worked in one movement

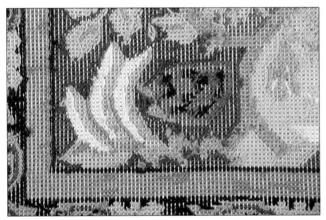

The back of a cross-stitch rug showing the short stitch on the back

The back of a cross-stitch rug showing the long stitch on the back

119

CROSS STITCH ON LINEN

As linen is not an interlocked fabric, it is important that the stitches do not slide between the threads. To avoid this, cross stitch is normally worked over two intersections.

When calculating the eventual size of your work, remember that stitching across two intersections of 28# count linen will give the same finished design size as stitching across one intersection of 14# canvas.

GOBELIN FILLING

This gives a pleasant padded look to a background. It was used in the Owls and Rabbits pillows. Where the background meets the main design, the stitches need to be shortened accordingly. Also, of course, at the top and bottom the "fill-in" stitches will be over two threads of the canvas, not four. It is extremely simple and quick; however, you will need more threads to cover the canvas than you use for tent stitch. Try adding one extra thread of crewel yarn – if it does not cover, put in another – until you are satisfied the canvas will not show through.

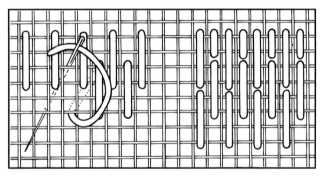

GOBELIN FILLING

BACKGROUND FOR BIRD & LEAF (page 108) This is exactly like gobelin filling, although I decided to go over three threads: make two stitches next to each other, then step down for one stitch, step down again for the next two, then up for the next two, and up for the next two, giving a wavy effect. One row was stitched using one color and the next a mixture of two.

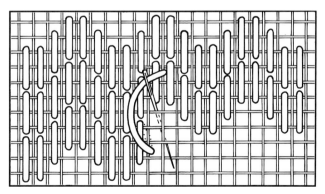

GOBELIN FILLING worked over 3 threads

STRETCHING

When the happy day arrives – the last stitch has been placed . . . the thread made secure . . . you view your finished work – you are only part-way to the full satisfaction that you are going to achieve. Whether or not your work of art is out of shape (and very few are not), it will genuinely benefit from stretching or blocking.

My firm belief is that this is a much more difficult thing to do than many people think. A professionally stretched pillow cover will have absolutely straight sides and perfectly right-angled corners. However, here are the principles; with quite a bit of practice, you may reach a high standard. Incidentally, linen is normally stitched on a frame; gentle ironing on the wrong side with the linen resting on a padded board is all that should be necessary.

Canvas is a pliable medium; the act of stitching can, and usually does, pull it out of shape. Diagonal stitches are most likely to do this. Stretching serves two purposes: the first is to return the canvas to its original shape, the second is to give the worked piece a crisp, nicely finished look – much as ironing will improve the look of a tablecloth even if it is only slightly creased. Just ironing your canvas will not give the same effect, however.

There is now special equipment available for stretching. There are stretcher boards which consist of a square of board marked with lines and drilled with holes at regular intervals and supplied with stainless steel nails. There are also racking machines which have pins that grip the edges of the canvas and will pull it out until straight, and I am sure there is other equipment that I have not heard of. If you do not have any of these, you need a clean board into which you can hammer nails (and remove them fairly easily). It has to be larger than the piece you are stretching. You also need carpet tacks or stainless steel nails, pliers, a hammer, a T-square, and a great deal of determination!

All pieces are stretched square or rectangular – not cut into any special shape. A template, if you have one, can be used to check the shape as you stretch.

Cut the selvage off your worked piece, and stitch a narrow hem all around by machine. The hem must be strong, as it is where you will put the nails or tacks.

If the piece is not very much out of shape, it can be easier to handle dry. If it needs dampening, I find that wrapping it in a wet dishtowel for a few minutes is easiest; do not soak. In case the board contains anything that might run onto the damp canvas, it should be covered securely with blotting paper or a clean cloth.

The aim is to tack the worked piece, right side down, onto the board so that all the canvas threads are running straight and at right angles to each other. It is called "stretching" simply because you will not achieve this unless you do stretch the canvas (and stretch it quite hard). People have favorite ways of placing the tacks; they need to be about ½ inch (1.25 cm) apart, or closer. If you have marked the centers of each side of the canvas and have a way of lining them up on the board (by measuring or pre-marking), you can nail the four centers or the corners. Or, you can start with one side and its adjacent side and continue around. You will almost certainly need to remove the tacks continually and replace them until you are happy that the piece is absolutely square and very taut. If you have not pulled it enough, it will just bubble out of shape again as it dries. If you did not dampen beforehand, or even if you did, you can lay a damp cloth on top of the piece and very lightly iron over it (do not press). This steams the work and, if it is dry, helps it move into the new shape. The drying is what sets it. It is absolutely essential that the piece is left until it is totally dry, which will be at least 24 hours (48 hours is safer).

There are varying viewpoints on the use of coatings to make the work hold its shape after being made up. If your stitching is likely to be subjected to any damp surroundings, it will start to return to its original stitched shape before being stretched; this would be a strong reason to use a weak solution of antifungicidal wallpaper paste on the back to help hold it. Other preparations are sold for this purpose; check with your needlework supplier or a local picture framer who knows about finishing needlework. Many embroidery stores can arrange stretching and finishings, so it is always worth asking. They can probably show you samples of what they have done and discuss your particular project with you.

You should now understand why you needed the extra unworked canvas all around your stitching. If you do not, for some reason, have enough, then strong cloth tape can be machine-stitched around the edges (preferably before working) to take the place of the excess canvas.

ASSEMBLING

I often feel that, after all the efforts of stitching, a special finish done by a professional seems a small investment. However, here are some basic directions if you prefer to do it yourself.

PILLOWS
Pillows come in an almost endless variety of shapes and sizes. Those in this book are piped, corded, or have an inset. Jasmine (page 61) is an example of what I call an inset, but it's a cheat! The stitched model was stretched, trimmed, and slipstitched onto the center of one side of a ready-made pillow cover before the filling was added.

For the corded pillows, you will need a filling 10 percent larger than the stitched area of canvas, and a backing material 2 inches (5 cm) larger – I like velvet or heavy silk – and a cord to fit all the way around the pillow plus ½ yard (0.5 meter) extra for knots or twists if you want them. Trim the stretched canvas to about 1 inch (2.5 cm) all around. Place this and the backing material right sides facing, and

baste carefully on three sides and along part of the fourth side, taking in each corner. With the stitching facing you, machine-stitch following your basting, keeping as close to your stitching line as possible. If you lightly hand-sew the canvas edges back and miter the corners, it will give your pillow a better shape. Turn right side out. Hand-sew the cord in place, knotting the corners as you go, and make sure that the corners are pulled right out. Insert the pad. Slipstitch the gap at the bottom.

For pillows piped with the backing fabric, you will need plain piping cord long enough to go around the pillow plus 1 inch (2.5 cm) for joining and enough extra backing fabric to enable you to cut strips on the bias (diagonally across the fabric) 2 inches (5 cm) wide and long enough to cover all the cord. The strips have to be cut on the bias, as the fabric will stretch in that direction and allow you to form the corners of the pillow without bunching. Trim the worked canvas 1 inch (2.5 cm) outside your stitching all around; cut the backing fabric to the same size. Cut the strips of fabric for piping. Join them, also on the bias, by machine-stitching them. Baste the piping fabric neatly around to cover the cord; place the covered cord between the embroidery and the backing fabric as they lie right sides facing. The piping must be on the "inside," out of sight. Baste very carefully so that the piping will lie tight up against your embroidery. Baste around the top, both sides, and along the bottom a little way after turning the corners. Leave a space in the middle of the bottom to insert the pad. If you have a piping or zipper foot, you can machine-stitch following your basting; otherwise, a careful backstitch by hand will give a good finish. Turn the cover right side out, and make sure the corners are square. Insert the pad and slipstitch the opening on the bottom edge to finish it.

RUGS

As already stated, all canvas work benefits from stretching, even if it is not really out of shape. If you are not going to have this done professionally, you will need a large board or old table or wooden floor that you do not mind making holes in. Failing that, you can press the work lightly with a steam iron on the reverse side. I must be honest and confess that not all my rugs have been stretched, but they are straight and soft and comfortable.

Many rug makers like to give their rugs a good finish by turning under the unworked canvas and making the last row of stitches around the outside of the rug through the two layers. This does give a very neat edge, but it makes stretching impossible – so stretch yours before this stage.

LINING Rugs that are intended as wallhangings or throws for sofas need a much lighter lining than those that will be walked on. For a light lining, you need strong thread, a long, strong, sharp needle, and a suitable lining fabric, perhaps something you might use for heavy curtains. For a heavy lining, you need a thin but firm, good-quality felt for interlining and a stronger outer lining such as burlap, Union cloth, or Holland. The felt should be exactly the same size as the worked area of the rug. The other linings need an extra 4–6 inches (10–15 cm) so that 2–3 inches (5–7 cm) can be turned under all around.

First trim the excess canvas all around the rug to within 2–3 inches (5–7.5 cm) of the worked area. Pinch it firmly back so that no raw canvas shows on the right side of the rug – pin and secure it with herringbone stitch. The corners will lie flatter if they are mitered. Now attach the fringe (see below). All the linings need to be secured in the center of the rug to prevent them from slipping or sagging. Pin each in place in turn and secure by stab stitching along the central line lengthwise and crosswise at intervals as frequently as you feel is necessary depending on the weight of the lining and the size of the rug. Pin around the edge, turning in the lining appropriately and slip stitch. Repeat if necessary with the felt and then the outer lining. There is no need to turn the felt under as it will not fray and would make too thick an edge.

FRINGING This is absolutely a matter of taste. Fringe can be omitted altogether, done in wool or cotton thread, and made as simple or elaborate as you like. The two rugs shown were both fringed with a strong cotton weft.

The quantity of fringe you will need can be calculated by counting the number of stitches across the width of the rug, multiplying by two and multiplying by twice the length of fringe that you intend. If you want to experiment with knotting or plaiting, you will need more.

Decide on the length of the fringe. Then cut a long piece of cardboard with a width that is slightly larger than the length of the fringe, and wind the fringing cord around the cardboard. Cut lengthwise in a straight line with a craft knife, and you will have fringe all the right length.

ATTACHING THE FRINGE The basic principle is very simple. It is just like threading a baggage tag. If you could fold the one thread of fringe in half and thread the loop through the edge of the canvas from back to front, you would then need only to tuck the two loose ends through the loop and pull. However, the difficulty is getting the folded thread through the canvas hole, which already contains your stitching. The quickest method is to use a latch hook, passing it through from front to back, hooking the double thread, and pulling it through to the front; the hook can be used to pull the two loose ends through the loop, tightening the knot by hand. If you do not have a latch hook, a needle large enough to take the double thread will do, but it is not as quick. If you make the fringe by threading in the other direction, you will find that from the front you have two straight pieces of fringe with no joining loop at the top. This, too, is a matter of personal taste.

Knotting fringes can be extremely complex and great fun – but you will need a different book!

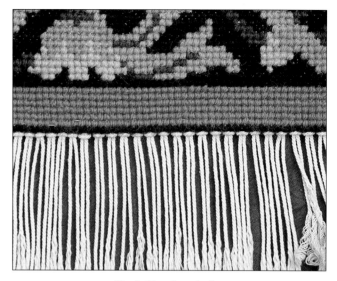
Simple fringe from the front

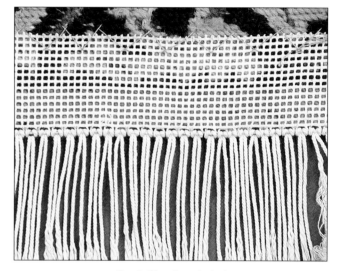
Simple fringe from the back

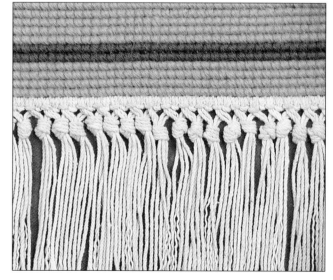
Slightly more complex fringe

NUMBER OF APPLETON THREADS IN THE NEEDLE

CANVAS	TENT STITCH	CROSS STITCH	STRAIGHT STITCH
18#/inch 7#/cm	2 crewel		3 crewel or 1 tapestry
14#/inch 5·5#/cm	2 crewel or 3 crewel or 1 tapestry		4 crewel
12#/inch 5#/cm	3 crewel or 1 tapestry		5 crewel or 6 crewel
8#/inch★ 3#/cm	6 crewel or 2 tapestry	4 crewel or 1 tapestry	8 crewel or 3 tapestry
6#/inch★ 2·5#/cm		8 crewel or 2 tapestry	

NUMBER OF PATERNAYAN THREADS IN THE NEEDLE

CANVAS	TENT STITCH	CROSS STITCH	STRAIGHT STITCH
18#/inch 7#/cm	1 strand		2 strands
14#/inch 5·5#/cm	2 strands		3 strands
12#/inch 5#/cm	2 strands		3 strands
8#/inch★ 3#/cm	1 thread (3 strands)	2 strands	
6#/inch★ 2·5#/cm	4 strands	1 thread (3 strands)	

★ Tent stitch and straight stitch, although quite possible on these coarser canvases, both require a lot of threads in the needle.

To work tent stitch using Paternayan Persian yarn, you must divide each thread into three strands. A single strand of Paternayan is slightly thicker than one thread of Appleton Crewel Wool.

PATERNAYAN D NUMBER EQUIVALENTS

D211 = 930
D234 = 931
D275 = 932
D389 = 534
D419 = 495
D511 = 641
D522 = 662
D531 = 652
D546 = 665

WHERE TO BUY
KITS AND MATERIALS

USA

APPLETON YARNS AND DESIGNERS FORUM KITS
Rose Cottage, 209 Richmond Street, El Segundo, CA
90245

PATERNAYAN PERSIAN YARNS
Johnson's Creative Arts, 445 Main Street West,
Townsend, MA 01474

The following suppliers stock Appleton yarns and other
needlecraft materials:

POTPOURRI ETC.
PO Box 78, Redondo Beach, CA 90277

NEEDLEPOINT INC.
251 Post Street, San Francisco CA 94108

THE JOLLY NEEDLEWOMAN
5810 Kennett Pike, Centreville, DE 19807

NEEDLE WORKS LTD.
4041 Tulane Avenue, New Orleans, LA 70119

THE ELEGANT NEEDLE LTD.
7954 MacArthur Blvd., Cabin John, MD 20818

SIGN OF THE ARROW/1867 FOUNDATION
9740 Clayton Road, St. Louis, MO 63124

LOUISE'S NEEDLEWORK
45 North High Street, Dublin, OH 43017

EWE & I
24 North Merion Avenue, Bryn Mawr, PA 19010

METAMORPHOSIS INC.
1108 Tyne Blvd., Nashville, TN 37220

DAN'S FIFTH AVENUE
1520 Fifth Avenue, Canyon, TX 79015

CHAPARRAL
3701 West Alabama, Suite 370, Houston, TX 77027

UK

APPLETON YARNS
Appleton Bros Limited, Thames Works, Church Street,
Chiswick, London W4 2PE

PATERNA PERSIAN YARNS
PO Box 1, Ossett, West Yorkshire WF5 9SA

DANISH FLOWER THREADS
Staddles & Co., Langrish, Petersfield, Hants GU32 1RQ

DMC THREADS
Dunlicraft, Pullman Road, Wigston, Leics LE8 2DY

AUSTRALIA

APPLETON YARNS
Clifton H Joseph, 391–393 Little Lonsdale Street,
Melbourne, Victoria 3000

APPLETON YARNS, PATERNA PERSIAN YARNS AND DESIGNERS
FORUM KITS
Altamira, 34 Murphy Street, South Yarra, Victoria 3141

Other good needlepoint sources (particularly for Designers Forum kits):

FRANCE: Voisine, 12 rue de l'Eglise, 92200
Neuilly-sur-Seine

ITALY: Royal Blue Company, Strada Castelvecchio 40,
10024 Moncalieri (TO)

DENMARK: Danish Handicraft Guild, Glentevej 70B, DK-
2400 Copenhagen

SPAIN: Madial, Principe de Vergara 82, 28006 Madrid

JAPAN: Yamanashi Hemslojd, 2–3–5 Kakinokizaka,
Meguro-ku, Tokyo

PLACES TO VISIT

USA

Abby Aldrich Rockefeller Folk Art Center
307 S. England Street
Williamsburg, Virginia 23187

Art Institute of Chicago
Michigan Avenue at Adams Street
Chicago, Illinois 60603

Cooper-Hewitt Museum
2 East 91st Street
New York, New York 10128

Fine Art Museums of San Francisco
M. H. de Young Memorial Museum
Golden Gate Park
San Francisco, California 94118

Metropolitan Museum of Art
5th Avenue at 82nd Street
New York, New York 10028

National History of American History
Science, Technology and Culture
Smithsonian Institution
Washington, D.C. 20560

Old Sturbridge Village
1 Old Sturbridge Village Road
Sturbridge, Massachusetts 01566

The Textile Museum
2320 S Street, N.W.
Washington, D.C. 20008

Witte Museum
3801 Broadway
San Antonio, Texas 78299

UK

Original works from the Arts & Crafts Movement are housed in the following places in the UK. Many are public museums or galleries with regular opening times. Others are collections either in the care of official bodies (such as the National Trust, the Society of Antiquaries, and the Richmond Fellowship) or in private homes; these are only viewable on special dates or by written appointment.

BEDFORD – Cecil Higgins Museum
BEXLEYHEATH – Red House
BIRMINGHAM – City Museum & Art Gallery
BRISTOL – Museum & Art Gallery
CAMBRIDGE – Fitzwilliam Museum
CAMBRIDGE – Jesus College
CAMBRIDGE – Queen's College
CARDIFF – Welsh Folk Museum
CARDIFF – Castle
CHELTENHAM – Art Gallery and Museums
EAST GRINSTEAD – Standen
HARTLEBURY CASTLE – Hereford & Worcester County Museum
IRONBRIDGE – Jackfield Tile Museum
LECHLADE – Kelmscott Manor
LEICESTER – County Museum & Art Gallery
LONDON – (Hammersmith) Kelmscott House*
LONDON – (Kensington) 8 Addison Road
LONDON – (Kensington) Leighton House
LONDON (Kensington) Linley Sambourne House
LONDON – (Kensington) Victoria & Albert Museum
LONDON – (Walthamstow) William Morris Gallery
MANCHESTER – Whitworth Art Gallery
NORWICH – Castle Museum
OXFORD – Oxford Union
SWANSEA – Brangwyn Hall
UXBRIDGE – Arthur Sanderson (Archive)
WOLVERHAMPTON – Wightwick Manor

* Kelmscott House is the headquarters of the William Morris Society, which has an active program of lectures, visits, study days, and social events, as well as a newsletter and journal. Membership applications should be addressed to Kelmscott House, 26 Upper Mall, London W6 9TA, England.

BIBLIOGRAPHY

Adburgham, Alison *Liberty's – A Biography of a Shop* (George Allen & Unwin, 1975)

Anscombe, Isabelle *Arts and Crafts Style* (Phaidon Oxford, 1991)

Anscombe, Isabelle & Charlotte Gere *Arts and Crafts in Britain and America* (Academy Editions, 1978)

Austwick, J & B *The Decorated Tile* (Pitman House, 1980)

Catleugh, Jon *William De Morgan Tiles* (Trefoil Books, 1983)

Clark, Fiona *William Morris – Wallpapers and Chintzes* (St Martin's Press/Academy Editions, 1973)

Coote, Stephen *William Morris – His Life and Work* (Garamond, 1990)

Dore, Helen *William Morris* (Pyramid Books, 1990)

Durant, Stuart *The Decorative Designs of C.F.A. Voysey* (The Lutterworth Press, 1990)

Fairclough, Oliver & Emmeline Leary *Textiles by William Morris and Morris & Co 1861–1940* (Thames and Hudson, 1981)

Gillow, Norah *William Morris – Designs and Patterns* (Bracken Books, 1988)

Greenwood, Martin *The Designs of William De Morgan* (Dennis and Wiltshire, 1989)

Naylor, Gillian *The Arts & Crafts Movement* (Studio Vista, 1980)

Naylor, Gillian *William Morris By Himself* (Macdonald Orbis, 1988)

Parry, Linda *Textiles of the Arts & Crafts Movement* (Thames & Hudson, 1988)

Parry, Linda *William Morris and the Arts & Crafts Movement* (Studio Editions, 1989)

Parry, Linda *William Morris Textiles* (Weidenfeld & Nicolson, 1983)

Poulson, Christine *William Morris* (Apple Press, 1989)

Vallance, Aymer *The Art of William Morris* (Dover, 1990)

Vallance, Aymer *The Life and Work of William Morris* (Studio Editions, 1986)

Watkinson, Ray *William Morris as Designer* (Studio Vista, 1967)

Wilhide, Elizabeth *William Morris – Decor and Design* (Pavilion, 1991)

ACKNOWLEDGMENTS

To acknowledge fully all the help that I have had in producing this book is impossible. There are, however, many people who deserve special mention, often for performing even more roles than they were originally asked to fill.

My husband Peter not only gave me confidence and advice but together with the rest of our family – particularly Nick, Paul and Julie – allowed me the time and space that I needed by keeping Designers Forum alive and well. Thanks also to daughter-in-law Sam and my brother Roy Haynes for constant encouragement. Plus, Appleton Brothers for their usual colorful service, Simon Deighton for his excellent and reliable printing, Sheila Thom for making tidiness out of chaos, Jean and Frank Dittrich in California, and Lawton Cooke in Australia for continuous support – they all enabled the business to carry on without me.

The finished pieces in the book would not be there without the artistic abilities of Phyllis and Robert Steed and the superb stitching of Selina Winter, Angela Kahan, Jean Cook, and Dorothy Vernon.

The genuinely pretty, as well as practical, charts demonstrate the technical skills of Ethan Danielson; Maggi McCormick deserves special appreciation for wrestling so tactfully with my verbal ramblings; Brenda Morrison is responsible for the elegant design of the whole book. The beautiful photographs are due to the skill of John Greenwood. His understanding of my work and his constant enthusiasm have made the hunting for locations and the photographic sessions great fun. He and I were helped in no small way by the styling of Andrea Spencer, Kes Seeberg and Dilys Williams, and by the good humor and imagination of his assistant, Quentin Harriott.

For the loan of their homes, furniture, or props, I would like to thank Michael and Gaynor Wilson, Oliver and his parents, Caroline Perry at The Tapestry Centre, Jane Chapman of Campden Needlecraft, John Masterson, Mikiko Yamanashi and Jean Wells. For special locations and loan of photographs, my thanks to Linda Howarth of The Richmond Fellowship (8 Addison Road), Matthew Wise of Markheath Securities (Stanmore Hall), Norah Gillow at The William Morris Gallery and – at Arthur Sanderson & Sons – Lesley Hoskins at their archive and Elizabeth Machin in the press office.

Finally, I acknowledge the patience of Vivienne Wells at David & Charles; her faith in me is more appreciated than she knows. Many of the individuals that I have mentioned are now personal friends; that is the pleasure and privilege of working with talented people. I want to thank them all for their inspiration and enthusiasm.

*The highly individual and untutored
efforts of my husband in 1973!*

INDEX